Plant-Based AIR FRYER —Cookbook—

365 DAYS OF QUICK, HEALTY AND DELICIOUS RECIPES TO MAKE EASY, TASTY AND BALANCED LIFESTYLE. INCLUDES A 100 DAILY MEAL PLAN!

ADAM RYE

© Copyright 2023 - All rights reserved by Adam Rye

COPYRIGHT PROTECTION WARNING

The author has registered this work at ProtectMyWork.com

Copyright Protected with www.ProtectMyWork.com, Reference Number: 21223190623S031

The content contained within this book may not be reproduced, duplicated or transmitted without direct written permission from the author or the publisher.

Under no circumstances will any blame or legal responsibility be held against the publisher, or author, for any damages, reparation, or monetary loss due to the information contained within this book, either directly or indirectly.

Legal Notice:

This book is copyright protected. It is only for personal use. You cannot amend, distribute, sell, use, quote or paraphrase any part, or the content within this book, without the consent of the author or publisher.

Disclaimer Notice:

Please note the information contained within this document is for educational and entertainment purposes only. All effort has been executed to present accurate, up to date, reliable, complete information. No warranties of any kind are declared or implied. Readers acknowledge that the author is not engaged in the rendering of legal, financial, medical or professional advice. The content within this book has been derived from various sources. Please consult a licensed professional before attempting any techniques outlined in this book.

By reading this document, the reader agrees that under no circumstances is the author responsible for any losses, direct or indirect, that are incurred as a result of the use of the information contained within this document, including, but not limited to, errors, omissions, or inaccuracies.

Credits:

Thanks to Margaret Jaszowska on Unsplash, Yashaswita Bhoir on Unsplash, Joseph Gonzalez on Unsplash, Kalisha Ocheni on Unsplash.

Cover images by iMarzi on DepositPhotos, Joseph Gonzalez on Unsplash.

All the images are generated by Artificial Intelligence.

The Author

Adam Rye was born in 1988 and grew up with his family in a beautiful rural countryside home.

Since he was a child, he loved the lifestyle surrounded by nature and as he grew up and studied engineering, he dedicated himself to studying plant-based cooking and writing recipes.

This plant-based diet brought him to good health and weight loss, and he then decided to publish his recipes.

Now he enjoys excellent health and has decided to share all his knowledge and delicious recipes with the public.

Today, Adam has a beautiful family: he has been married for six years and has two daughters. He still lives in the countryside home where his family can enjoy the benefits of living away from the chaos of cities.

CONTENTS

19
BREAKFAST

40
SNACKS AND APPETIZERS

61
MAIN DISHES

82
SIDES AND SALADS

103
DESSERTS

TABLE OF CONTENTS

INTRODUCTION 11
Benefits of Air Fryer Cooking 11
Essential Tools and Ingredients for Plant-Based Air Fryer Cooking 16
Stocking a Plant-Based Air Fryer Pantry 17
Recommended Plant-Based Air Fryer Pantry List 17

CHAPTER 1
BREAKFAST 19
1. Avocado Toast with Vegan Feta Cheese 21
2. Pancakes with Blueberries 22
3. Sweet Potato Hash with Kale and Chickpeas 23
4. French Toast with Berry Compote 24
5. Burrito with Tofu Scramble 25
6. Quesadilla with Spinach and Mushroom 26
7. Sausage Patties 27
8. Sandwiches with Veggie Bacon 28
9. Waffles with Fresh Fruit 29
10. Potatoes with Rosemary and Garlic 30
11. Baked Oatmeal with Nuts and Dried Fruit 31
12. Stuffed Peppers with Quinoa and Black Beans 32
13. Breakfast Casserole with Tofu and Vegetables 33
14. Tacos with Tofu Scramble and Salsa 34
15. Strata with Grilled Veggies 35
16. Sweet Potato Waffles with Maple Syrup 36
17. Bake with Tofu and Broccoli 37
18. Frittata with Spinach and Tomatoes 38
19. French Toast Casserole with Cinnamon and Maple Syrup 39
20. Bowl with Tofu Scramble and Roasted Veggies 40

CHAPTER 2
SNACKS AND APPETIZERS 41
21. Sweet Potato Fries with Rosemary and Sea Salt 42
22. Onion Rings with Spicy Dipping Sauce 43
23. Zucchini Chips with Parmesan and Herbs 44
24. Falafel with Tahini Sauce 45
25. Carrot Fries with Curry Powder and Coconut Oil 46
26. Spring Rolls with Sweet and Sour Sauce 47
27. Portobello Mushroom Caps with Balsamic Glaze 48
28. Tofu Bites with Buffalo Sauce and Ranch Dipping Sauce 49

29. Brussels Sprouts with Balsamic Vinegar and Honey 50
30. Cauliflower Wings with Barbecue Sauce 51
31. Sweet and Spicy Peppers with Vinegar and Honey 52
32. Artichoke Hearts with Lemon and Garlic 53
33. Spiced Chickpeas with Cumin and Paprika 54
34. Stuffed Jalapenos with Cream Cheese and Chives 55
35. Baked Sweet Potato Rounds with Cinnamon and Maple Syrup 56
36. Eggplant Parmesan Bites with Marinara Sauce and Vegan Cheese 57
37. Roasted Garlic with Olive Oil and Sea Salt 58
38. Fried Rice Balls with Vegetables and Tamari 59
39. Spiced Nuts with Cayenne and Maple Syrup 60
40. Baked Mac and Cheese Bites with Panko Breadcrumbs 61

CHAPTER 3
MAIN DISHES 62

41. Tofu and Vegetable Stir-Fry with Sesame Oil and Soy Sauce 63
42. Sweet Potato and Black Bean Tacos with Avocado Cream Sauce 64
43. Chickpea Curry with Coconut Milk and Spices 65
44. Quinoa and Vegetable Bowl with Lemon and Olive Oil 66
45. Ratatouille with Tomato Sauce and Herbs 67
46. Roasted Vegetable and Rice Casserole with Vegan Cheese 68
47. Teriyaki Tofu and Vegetables with Rice 69
48. Cauliflower Steaks with Romesco Sauce and Almonds 70
49. Mushroom and Onion Pizzas with Vegan Cheese and Herbs 71
50. Sweet Potato and Kale Enchiladas with Red Sauce and Vegan Cheese 72
51. Pad Thai with Rice Noodles and Peanut Sauce 73
52. Zucchini and Tomato Gratin with Cheese and Herbs 74
53. BBQ Tofu and Vegetable Skewers with Barbecue Sauce 75
54. Stuffed Bell Peppers with Quinoa, Black Beans and Cheese 76
55. Lentil and Vegetable Shepherd's Pie with Mashed Potatoes 77
56. Grilled Cheese Sandwich 78
57. Seitan and Vegetable Skewers with Lemon and Herbs 79
58. Butternut Squash and Sage Lasagna with Vegan Cheese 80
59. Chickpea and Vegetable Burgers with Buns and Fixings 81
60. Stuffed Portobello Mushrooms with Quinoa, Spinach and Vegan Cheese 82

CHAPTER 4
SIDES AND SALADS 83
61. Roasted Carrots with Honey and Thyme 84
62. Grilled Corn on the Cob with Chili Powder and Lime 85
63. Baked Potato Wedges with Rosemary and Sea Salt 86
64. Roasted Brussels Sprouts with Balsamic Vinegar and Maple Syrup 87
65. Sweet Potato Fries with Garlic Aioli 88
66. Grilled Asparagus with Lemon and Olive Oil 89
67. Cauliflower Rice with Turmeric and Cumin 90
68. Roasted Butternut Squash with Cinnamon and Maple Syrup 91
69. Baked Sweet Potato with Cinnamon and Coconut Oil 92
70. Grilled Zucchini with Balsamic Vinegar and Basil 93
71. Fried Rice with Vegetables and Soy Sauce 94
72. Roasted Bell Peppers with Oregano and Garlic 95
73. Quinoa Salad with Avocado, Cilantro, and Lime 96
74. Grilled Eggplant with Balsamic Vinegar and Mint 97
75. Coleslaw with Vegan Mayo and Vinegar 98
76. Pasta Salad with Vegetables and Vinaigrette 99
77. Grilled Peaches with Cinnamon and Honey 100
78. Potato Salad with Vegan Mayo and Herbs 101
79. Roasted Radishes with Butter and Sea Salt 102
80. Roasted Beets with Orange and Thyme 103

CHAPTER 5
DESSERTS 104
81. Apple Chips with Cinnamon and Sugar 105
82. Peach Crisp with Oats and Brown Sugar 106
83. Baked Banana Bread with Walnuts and Cinnamon 107
84. Grilled Pineapple with Coconut Sugar and Lime Juice 108
85. Cinnamon Sugar Donut Holes with Powdered Sugar 109
86. Baked Blueberry Muffins with Almond Flour and Maple Syrup 110
87. Sweet Potato Pie with Coconut Oil and Maple Syrup 111
88. Grilled Peaches with Vanilla Ice Cream and Caramel Sauce 112
89. Cinnamon sugar donuts 113
90. Strawberry Rhubarb Crumble with Almond Flour and Coconut Sugar 114
91. Baked Apple Fritters with Cinnamon and Sugar 115
92. Cinnamon Sugar Churros with Chocolate Sauce 116
93. Grilled Nectarines with Ice Cream and Berry Sauce 117

94. Baked Peach Cobbler with Oats and Coconut Sugar 118
95. Grilled Plums with Ice Cream and Balsamic Glaze 119
96. Cinnamon Sugar Apple Rings with Caramel Dip 120
97. Baked Banana Bread with Chocolate Chips and Walnuts 121
98. Strawberry Sorbet with Coconut Milk and Sugar 122
99. Grilled Pears with Vanilla Ice Cream and Honey 123
100. Baked Cinnamon Sugar Donuts with Chocolate Glaze 124
101. Grilled Mangoes with Ice Cream and Coconut Milk 125

100 DAILY MEAL PLAN 126

MEASUREMENT CONVERSION 134

INDEX OF RECIPES 135

CONCLUSION 137
Tips for Successful Plant-Based Air Fryer Cooking 137
Final Thoughts 138

Introduction

Diets based on plant-derived foods are gaining traction as people pursue better well-being and more eco-friendly lifestyles. The Air Fryer is a versatile appliance, ideal for preparing a variety of tasty and nutritious dishes. With the Plant-Based Air Fryer Cookbook, we bring together the best of both worlds, offering a wealth of delicious, plant-based recipes that are easy to make and perfectly suited to the Air Fryer. This book is the ideal tool for anyone looking to include more plant-based meals in their diet, whether they are vegan, vegetarian, or simply want to reduce their meat intake.

In this all-inclusive recipe book, you'll find 100 delectable and healthy dishes crafted to please the palate and provide essential nutrients. From breakfast to snacks and appetizers, to main dishes, sides, salads, and even desserts, this cookbook has everything you need to create a complete, plant-based meal plan. Are you starting on your cooking adventure or do you already know your way around the kitchen? Beginner or expert, these easy-to-follow recipes will let you enjoy the best of your Air Fryer's food.

One of the greatest benefits of the Air Fryer is that you can cook healthier versions of your favorite foods. The high-speed air circulation system cooks food evenly, reducing the need for oil and making your meals lower in fat and calories. Whether you are cooking up crispy tofu, roasting sweet potatoes, or whipping up a luscious dessert, the Air Fryer is the perfect tool to help you create delicious, healthy meals, sure to satisfy you.

So, whether you want to take your plant-based cooking to the next level or are looking for a collection of delicious, healthy recipes that are easy to make, the Plant-Based Air Fryer Cookbook is your answer. With its comprehensive collection of recipes, easy-to-follow instructions, and clear, step-by-step photographs, this book will help you create mouth-watering, plant-based meals sure to become family favorites.

Benefits of Air Fryer Cooking

Air Fryers have become popular kitchen appliances because of the unique cooking method using circulating hot air. Not only is air fryer cooking a more health-conscious option than conventional deep-frying, but other advantages also make it a solid choice for those seeking to add to their culinary know-how.

Possibly, the best benefit of air fryer cooking is it allows you to cook your food with much less oil. The hot air circulation ensures uniform cooking, resulting in a crunchy outer layer while keeping the interior tender and succulent. As a result, the food turns out healthier and significantly tastier. Also, using the air fryer is quick and simple. Since it can prepare meals in just a few minutes, it is an excellent choice for people with limited time who want a scrumptious dish. And then, air fryers are incredibly easy to use and clean, making them a great option for anyone looking to minimize the time and effort involved in cooking.

Ultimately, using an air fryer is a greener option than conventional deep-frying techniques. Since it requires minimal oil, it creates less waste and is an eco-friendly approach to food preparation. Adopting this method is a brilliant decision for those who want to minimize their ecological impact and aid the environment.

To sum up, air fryer cooking offers a wide range of benefits, from being healthier and more convenient to being more environmentally friendly. If you're a busy professional or simply looking for a healthier way to cook, air fryer cooking is definitely worth considering.

Health Benefits

Firstly, air fryers cook food with minimal oil, reducing the amount of unhealthy saturated fats and trans fats in your diet. Unlike traditional deep frying, which completely immerses the food in oil, air fryers only require a small amount of added oil. This oil is then evenly circulated to cook the food. The result is lower calories, fewer fats, and less oil, making it a healthier cooking method.

Secondly, With air fryer cooking, the nutrients stay in the food. Traditional deep-frying causes food to lose nutritional value. Vitamins and minerals are lost because of high temperatures and long cooking times. On the other hand, air fryers cook food with much less heat, preserving the nutrients, and making it easier to maintain a healthy diet.

Thirdly, air fryers reduce the risk of cardiovascular disease, as they produce fewer harmful compounds, such as acrylamides, when cooking food. Acrylamides occur naturally. They are elements produced when foods are cooked at high temperatures and are known to increase the risk of cardiovascular disease. Because air fryers can cook food at lower temperatures, the production of these harmful compounds is reduced, for safer and healthier cooking.

> **HEALTH BENEFITS**
> - Reduced Oil and Fat Content
> - Improved Nutrient Retention
> - Reduced Risk of Chronic Diseases
> - Enhanced Food Safety

Greater Convenience

No more long hours in the kitchen. The air fryer will cook your food much faster than a traditional oven. It can be especially helpful when you're looking to prepare a quick and healthy meal. With the air fryer, you can cook a variety of plant-based foods, such as vegetables, tofu, and even plant-based meat alternatives, in a matter of minutes.

Clean-up after cooking is often a tedious and time-consuming part of meal prep. However, air fryers are very easy to clean, and they don't require much scrubbing or soaking. Simply wipe down the interior with a damp cloth and you're done.

With an air fryer, food cooks evenly and consistently, meaning you can rely on them to produce great results every time. Whether you're cooking a single serving or fixing a meal for a crowd, the air fryer is a reliable and convenient option for plant-based cooking.

An air fryer is versatile. They are great for

cooking a variety of plant-based foods, including vegetables, tofu, and even plant-based meat alternatives. With an air fryer, you have a wonderful tool for creating different, nutrient-dense plant-based meals.

Air fryers promote healthy cooking: By reducing the amount of oil needed, air fryers allow you to enjoy delicious, healthy, and guilt-free plant-based meals. This is particularly crucial for individuals who focus on their health and aim to follow a plant-based eating plan.

And, they're space-saving: Air fryers boast a small footprint, require minimal countertop space, and are an excellent choice for those with smaller kitchen areas. Regardless of whether you're preparing meals for yourself or a family, air fryers give a convenient and space-efficient solution for plant-based cooking.

CONVENIENCE BENEFITS

- Quick and Easy Cooking
- Versatile Cooking Options
- Reduced Cooking Time
- Easy Clean-Up

Financial Benefits

Air fryers can even help your budget, especially if you follow a plant-based diet. Here are a few ways that air fryer cooking can save you money while also being a healthy, environmentally friendly option.

Air fryers cook food more evenly, reducing the risk of under or over-cooking, which can lead to food waste. This means you can save money by using all your ingredients, instead of throwing away partially cooked or burned food.

Plant-based diets usually rely on foods like beans, lentils, and whole grains, which are typically less expensive than meat. By air frying these ingredients, they become crispy and delicious, making it a great way to save money on your weekly grocery bill.

By using less energy than traditional ovens and stovetops, your air fryer can give you lower electric bills. This is especially important if you are cooking multiple times a day, as energy savings really add up over time.

The air fryer is handy and can cook many types of dishes, from appetizers to the main course. This means you don't have to purchase separate cooking tools for each dish, a real money saver in the long run.

FINANCIAL BENEFITS

- Reduces Energy Costs
- Lower Maintenance Costs
- Eliminates Expensive Cooking Oils

Environmental Benefits

There are many advantages to using an air fryer for plant-based cooking, but the environmental benefits are particularly significant.

You will reduce your energy use. Because air fryers are more energy-efficient than traditional ovens, you can reduce your carbon footprint. Heating and preparing meals with your air fryer uses less energy. This results in energy conservation and fewer greenhouse gas emissions. Unlike conventional ovens, which often need plenty of aluminum foil or parchment paper to stop food from sticking, air fryers let you minimize their use, particularly when preparing plant-based dishes. As a result, there's a reduction in the waste

14 / INTRODUCTION

produced and this encourages a more environmentally aware approach to cooking.

Most traditional cooking methods need a lot of water for preparation and cleaning up after a meal. With air fryer cooking, you save water by using less to wash your dishes. And, because air fryers need less water to clean than other cooking utensils, they are a more sustainable option.

> **ENVIRONMENTAL BENEFITS**
> - Reduces Carbon Footprint
> - Less Use of Non-Renewable Resources
> - Reduces Food Waste

Air Fryer Cooking Tips and Techniques

Air fryer cooking has taken the culinary world by storm, offering a healthier, more convenient, and environmentally friendly alternative to traditional frying methods. For those who follow a plant-based diet, air fryers are an excellent way to cook a wide range of delicious and nutritious foods without extra oil. Here, we'll explore some of the best air fryer cooking techniques and tips for creating healthy plant-based meals. From mastering the basics to discovering new and creative ways to use your air fryer, the following pages will help you make the most of this versatile kitchen appliance.

BEST FOODS FOR AIR FRYER COOKING

An air fryer is a great tool for cooking a variety of plant-based foods, but some foods are better for this cooking method than others. Here's a guide to some of the many plant-based foods best suited to cooking in an air fryer:

- **Tofu:** Tofu is a flexible ingredient that works well in many dishes, including stir-fries, salads, and sandwiches. When cooked in an air fryer, tofu develops a crisp exterior that is perfect for pairing with a variety of sauces and dips.
- **Root vegetables:** Cook root vegetables to crunchy perfection. Those mealtime staples like carrots, potatoes, and sweet potatoes, are delicious when cooked in the air fryer. They make great a side dish or can combine with other ingredients to create a hearty main course.
- **Frozen fruits and vegetables:** Keep frozen fruits and vegetables handy for quick and easy meals. When prepared in an air fryer, they develop a crispy exterior while still keeping their natural moisture and nutrients. Frozen vegetables, such as green beans and Brussels sprouts, make a delicious side dish, while frozen fruits, like strawberries and bananas, make wonderful snacks and desserts.
- **Legumes:** The humble legume is the star of many plant-based recipes. Chickpeas, lentils, and other legumes cooked in an air fryer develop a crispy exterior that is perfect for snacking or as a topping for salads and bowls.
- **Seitan:** A high-protein, plant-based meat substitute, seitan is often used in vegan and vegetarian cuisine. Cooking in an air fryer gives seitan a crispy exterior that is great for sandwiches, stir-fries, and more.

USING AN AIR FRYER FOR BEST RESULTS

Knowing how your air fryer works is important. They essentially circulate hot air around the food, which gives a crispy, fried-like texture without using large amounts of oil. This is great for plant-based cooking because it allows you to get delicious results without relying on animal products.

When using an air fryer for plant-based cooking, it's vital to choose the right foods. Moist foods like mushrooms or zucchini, can become soft and squashy in the air fryer. On the other hand, foods with low moisture content, such as potatoes or tofu, do well. Consider this when selecting your ingredients and consider the result you want to achieve.

For mealtime success, prepare the food correctly. Cutting the food into similar size pieces will help it cook evenly. It's a good idea to warm up your air fryer for several minutes before use for uniform cooking. Pay close attention to the time and heat settings, as some ingredients need different cooking conditions. Also, shaking the container every 10-15 minutes will guarantee the food cooks evenly and doesn't stick to the surface.

Tips for Successful Air Fryer Cooking

Getting the best results from your air fryer involves a few tips and techniques. Here are some essential tips for successful plant-based air fryer cooking:

- **Choose the Right Foods:** While you can cook almost anything in an air fryer, some foods work better than others. Vegetables like carrots, broccoli, and cauliflower cook well in the air fryer, as do plant-based proteins such as tofu and tempeh.
- **Cut Evenly:** For even cooking, it's important to cut your food into uniform, bite-sized pieces. When everything cooks at the same time, you won't end up with any burned or undercooked parts.
- **Preheat:** Don't forget to preheat your air fryer before cooking, it ensures that your food cooks evenly and helps prevent sticking.
- **Use Cooking Spray:** To prevent sticking and help the food cook evenly, it's important to spray your air fryer basket with cooking spray before starting.
- **Shake the Basket:** Shake the basket from time to time while cooking. This moves the food around, so it doesn't stick together and all sides get evenly cooked.
- **Use a Cooking Thermometer:** Using a cooking thermometer guarantees your food reaches the desired level of doneness, preventing undercooked or overcooked meals.

Essential Tools and Ingredients for Plant-Based Air Fryer Cooking

Air Fryer Cuisine: To get the best possible results, it's essential to have the proper equipment and ingredients readily available. Here is a list of the key tools and ingredients you need for plant-based air fryer cooking.

Tools:

- **Air Fryer:** The fundamental tool for air fryer cooking. It is vital to choose an air fryer with a large enough capacity to cook a meal for your family or guests.
- **Measuring Cups and Spoons:** These are essential to measure ingredients accurately.
- **Tongs:** Let you turn or remove food from the air fryer easily without burning your hands.
- **Baking Sheet:** To cook large batches of food in the air fryer.
- **Silicone Baking Mats:** Useful for stopping food from sticking to the air fryer basket, making clean-up easier.

Here are some favorite ingredients:

- **Sweet Potatoes:** This staple of plant-based cooking is versatile, nourishing, and delicious when air fried.
- **Black Beans:** A major source of plant-based protein, fiber, and iron. Black beans are a must-have ingredient for any plant-based air fryer meal.
- **Avocado:** A superfood loaded with healthy fats, fiber, and potassium. Avocado can be used in a variety of ways, from making guacamole to serving as a creamy taco sauce.
- **Plant-based Milk:** Used for making vegan sauces and dips, plant-based milk is an all-important ingredient for plant-based air fryer cooking.
- **Vegan Feta Cheese:** A delicious and nutritious alternative to traditional dairy-based cheese. Vegan feta cheese is an ingredient in many dishes, from salads to toast.

Stocking a Plant-Based Air Fryer Pantry

A well-stocked pantry allows you to quickly and easily rustle up a variety of meals without a trip to the grocery store. Here are a few tips to help you with stocking your plant-based air fryer pantry.

Start with whole foods. The basics of a plant-based diet are whole foods like fruits, vegetables, legumes, and whole grains. Keep a variety of produce on hand. Leafy greens, root vegetables, and seasonal fruits ensure you have many options for your air fryer meals. Have canned legumes, black beans, chickpeas, and lentils to add protein and fiber to your meals. Whole grains like quinoa, brown rice, and whole wheat pasta are just staples that are great to have handy as a base for air fryer meals.

Include plant-based proteins. Plant-based proteins, such as tofu, tempeh, and seitan, are versatile and are used in an assortment of dishes. Stock your pantry with these plant-based protein options and you'll always have a protein source available for your air fryer meals.

Seasonings and condiments. To add flavor to your air fryer meals, stock your pantry with a selection of seasonings and condiments. Cumin, chili powder, and oregano are just some of the all-important herbs and spices that add flavor to your dishes. Plant-based condiments such as hot sauce, salsa, and vegan mayo will also add a little extra zing to your air fryer meals.

Recommended Plant-Based Air Fryer Pantry List

When it comes to cooking delicious and healthy plant-based meals in an air fryer, having the right ingredients on hand is key. This is our recommended list of plant-based pantry staples you should stock in your kitchen to make the most of your air fryer cooking.

- **Grains:** Rice, quinoa, pasta, whole wheat flour, cornmeal, and other grains are primary staples in many plant-based diets. They are adaptable and can act as foundations for many meal options, like stir-fries, tacos, or soups.
- **Legumes:** Beans, lentils, chickpeas, and others, are excellent sources of protein and fiber, suitable for creating dishes like salads, spreads, and patties.
- **Nuts and seeds:** Almonds, walnuts, cashews, chia seeds, and more, are a rich source of beneficial fats and can be

used in various recipes, including nut spreads, energy bars, and baked treats.
- **Vegetables:** Bell peppers, onions, garlic, carrots, and other vegetables are the building blocks of any plant-based kitchen. These ingredients can be used to make many dishes, including stir-fry, roasted vegetables, and soups.
- **Fruits:** Apples, bananas, berries, and other fruits are a natural source of sweetness and can be used to make a medley of dishes, like smoothies, baked goods, and snacks.
- **Plant-based proteins:** Tofu, tempeh, and seitan are popular plant-based proteins that will make an array of dishes, such as stir-fry, tacos, and burgers.

CHAPTER 1

Breakfast

Special Announcement for Our Valued Readers!

Dear Reader,

I have some exciting news to share with you! I am thrilled to announce that I am currently working on a **brand new recipe book**, set to be released in September 2023. This upcoming book will be filled with more delicious and healthy plant-based recipes, just like the ones you've enjoyed in the "Plant-Based Air Fryer Cookbook."

Your support means the world to me, and **I would be incredibly grateful if you could leave a lovely review for my current book**. Your feedback helps inspire and motivate me to keep creating amazing content for you.

But that's not all! By subscribing to my newsletter, you'll have the chance to be selected as one of the lucky recipients of a **free copy of my upcoming book**.

Just scan the QR code below to join our community and be part of this exciting journey together.

Thank you for being an essential part of this incredible adventure. Your enthusiasm and encouragement drive me to deliver the best recipes for your healthy and delicious plant-based lifestyle.

Stay tuned for more updates, and I can't wait to share the next culinary adventure with you!

Happy Cooking,

Adam Rye

Avocado Toast with Vegan Feta Cheese

★ ☆ ☆ ☆ ☆

COOK TIME: 10 MINUTES

PREP TIME: 15 MINUTES

SERVINGS: 4

INGREDIENTS

- 4 slices of whole-grain bread
- 2 ripe avocados, pitted and peeled
- 1 cup vegan feta cheese, crumbled
- 1 tablespoon olive oil
- 1 tablespoon lemon juice
- 1/4 teaspoon sea salt
- 1/4 teaspoon ground black pepper
- 1/2 teaspoon red pepper flakes (optional)
- 2 tablespoons fresh cilantro, chopped

INSTRUCTIONS

1. Preheat your air fryer to 350°F (175°C). Lightly brush each slice of bread with olive oil on both sides.
2. Place the bread slices in the air fryer basket, making sure not to overlap them. Cook for 5 minutes, flipping halfway through, or until the bread is golden and crispy.
3. Mix the avocados until smooth in a bowl. Stir in the lemon juice, sea salt, and black pepper. Adjust seasoning to taste.
4. Spread the avocado mixture evenly onto the toasted bread slices.
5. Sprinkle the crumbled vegan feta cheese over the avocado layer.
6. Incorporate a smidgen of crushed red pepper on the summit for a fiery touch, should you desire it.
7. Garnish each toast with chopped cilantro and serve immediately.

Nutrition Information (per serving): Calories: 349, Fat: 23g, Carbohydrates: 29g, Protein: 9g, Fiber: 9g

Pancakes with Blueberries

★ ☆ ☆ ☆ ☆

COOK TIME:
10 MINUTES

PREP TIME:
15 MINUTES

SERVINGS:
6 PANCAKES

INGREDIENTS

- 1 1/2 cups all-purpose flour
- 3 1/2 tsp baking powder
- 1/2 tsp salt
- 1 tbsp granulated sugar
- 1 1/4 cups unsweetened almond milk
- 1 flax egg (1 tbsp ground flaxseed mixed with 2 1/2 tbsp water)
- 3 tbsp melted vegan butter
- 1 tsp vanilla extract
- 1 cup fresh blueberries
- Non-stick cooking spray

INSTRUCTIONS

1. In a large mixing bowl, whisk together the versatile flour, leavening agent, sodium chloride, and crystalline sweetener.
2. In a separate bowl, combine the unsweetened almond milk, prepared flax egg, melted vegan butter, and vanilla extract.
3. Slowly incorporate the liquid components into the dry ones, blending until they are evenly mixed. Avoid excessive stirring.
4. Tenderly integrate the fresh blueberries into the mixture.
5. Warm up your air fryer to 350°F. Use a non-stick spray on the air fryer's container.
6. Scoop about 1/4 cup of the pancake batter onto the prepared air fryer basket or tray, making sure to leave space between each pancake.
7. Prepare the pancakes by cooking them for roughly 5 minutes, or until the borders start to develop a golden hue. Flip the pancakes and proceed to cook until they are completely done, for a 5 minutes.
8. Take the pancakes out of the air fryer and proceed with the rest of the batter using the same method.
9. Serve the pancakes with your favorite vegan butter and maple syrup. You may also add a smidgen of crushed red pepper on the summit for a fiery touch, should you desire it.

Nutritional Facts (per pancake): 253 Calories, 8g Fat, 40g Carbohydrates, 5g Protein, 2g Fiber

Sweet Potato Hash with Kale and Chickpeas

★★☆☆☆

COOK TIME: 30 MINUTES

PREP TIME: 15 MINUTES

SERVINGS: 4

INGREDIENTS

- 2 medium sweet potatoes, peeled and diced
- 1 bunch kale, stems removed and chopped
- 1 can (15 ounces) chickpeas, drained and rinsed
- 1 small red onion, diced
- 2 cloves garlic, minced
- 2 tablespoons olive oil
- 1 teaspoon smoked paprika
- 1/2 teaspoon ground cumin
- Salt and pepper, to taste
- **Optional toppings:** avocado slices, fresh cilantro, hot sauce

INSTRUCTIONS

1. Preheat Air Fryer to 400°F.
2. In a large mixing bowl, combine diced sweet potatoes, chopped kale, chickpeas, diced onion, and minced garlic.
3. Drizzle the olive oil over the mixture and toss to coat evenly. Add smoked paprika, ground cumin, salt, and pepper, and mix well.
4. Distribute the blend evenly on a sizable baking tray, forming one layer for uniform cooking.
5. Roast for approximately 25-30 minutes, or when the sweet potatoes become soft and acquire a light golden hue, while stirring from time to time.
6. Remove from the oven and let it cool slightly. Taste and adjust seasoning if necessary.
7. Enjoy while hot, and feel free to garnish with additional options like sliced avocado, fresh coriander, or some spicy sauce.

Nutritional Facts (per serving): 357 Calories, 11g Fat, 55g Carbohydrates, 14g Protein, 13g Fiber

CHAPTER 1. BREAKFAST / 23

French Toast with Berry Compote

★★☆☆☆

COOK TIME: 12 MINUTES

PREP TIME: 10 MINUTES

SERVINGS: 4

INGREDIENTS

- 8 slices of day-old bread (preferably brioche or challah)
- 4 large eggs
- 1 cup almond milk (or any non-dairy milk)
- 1 tsp pure vanilla extract
- 1/2 tsp ground cinnamon
- 1/4 tsp ground nutmeg
- 2 tbsp maple syrup (for dipping)
- Non-stick cooking spray

Berry Compote:
- 2 cups mixed berries (fresh or frozen)
- 1/4 cup granulated sugar
- 1 tbsp lemon juice
- 1 tsp cornstarch
- 1 tbsp water

INSTRUCTIONS

1. Blend the eggs, almond milk, vanilla essence, cinnamon, and nutmeg using a whisk.
2. Dip each slice of bread into the egg mixture, ensuring both sides are coated evenly, then place them on a wire rack to allow excess mixture to drip off.
3. Begin by heating the air fryer to 375°F and applying non-stick spray to the air fryer basket.
4. Place the slices of bread within the basket, making certain that they form a single tier without any overlap.
5. Allow the bread to cook for 6 minutes, then cautiously turn the slices over using tongs or a spatula.
6. Continue cooking for 6 minutes. The French toast turns golden brown and crisp.
7. As the French toast cooks, prepare the berry compote by combining mixed berries, sugar, and lemon juice in a medium-sized saucepan over medium heat. Gently stir the mixture until the berries start to soften and the sugar melts, which should take about 5 minutes.
8. In a small bowl, whisk together cornstarch and water, then add it to the berry mixture and stir until thickened, about 2-3 minutes.
9. Should you desire, include a dollop of the berry compote and a trickle of maple syrup.

Nutrition Information (per serving): Calories: 335, Fat: 10g, Carbohydrates: 49g, Protein: 12g, Fiber: 4g

Burrito with Tofu Scramble

★ ☆ ☆ ☆ ☆

COOK TIME: 10 MINUTES

PREP TIME: 10 MINUTES

SERVINGS: 2

INGREDIENTS

- 1/2 block of extra-firm tofu
- 2 tablespoons of olive oil
- 1/4 teaspoon of garlic powder
- 1/4 teaspoon of cumin
- 1/4 teaspoon of turmeric
- 1/4 teaspoon of paprika
- Salt and pepper to taste
- 2 large flour tortillas
- 1/2 avocado, sliced
- Salsa, to taste
- Vegan cheese, shredded
- 1/4 cup of black beans

INSTRUCTIONS

1. Start by pressing extra-firm tofu to remove excess water.
2. Once you have cut the extra-firm tofu into small, bite-sized pieces, keep it aside.
3. Next, in a mixing bowl, blend olive oil, garlic powder, cumin, turmeric, paprika, salt, and pepper.
4. Add the cubed tofu pieces to the spice blend in the mixing bowl and toss until each piece is evenly coated. Next, preheat your air fryer to 380°F.
5. Preheat your air fryer to 380°F.
6. Place the well-seasoned tofu pieces in the air fryer basket and cook until crispy, which usually takes about 8-10 minutes. Ensure that you occasionally shake the basket to ensure that the tofu cooks evenly.
7. As the tofu is cooking, you can heat the tortillas in the microwave for 20 seconds to make them soft and pliable.
8. Once the tofu is cooked, assemble the burritos with the tofu scramble, sliced avocado, salsa, vegan cheese, and black beans.
9. Roll the tortilla tightly and place it in the air fryer basket. Cook for another 2-3 minutes until the burrito is crispy.
10. Serve hot and enjoy your flavorful and healthy Air Fryer Burrito with Tofu Scramble!

Nutrition Information (per serving): 467 Calories, 25g Fat, 44g Carbohydrates, 18g Protein, 8g Fiber

CHAPTER 1. BREAKFAST / 25

Quesadilla with Spinach and Mushroom

★ ☆ ☆ ☆ ☆

COOK TIME: 10 MINUTES

PREP TIME: 10 MINUTES

SERVINGS: 2

INGREDIENTS

- 4 medium tortillas
- 1 cup spinach, chopped
- 1 cup mushrooms, sliced
- 1/2 cup vegan cheese, shredded
- 1/4 cup red onion, thinly sliced
- 2 tablespoons olive oil
- Salt and pepper, to taste

INSTRUCTIONS

1. Preheat the air fryer to 400°F (200°C).
2. In a skillet, heat olive oil over medium heat. Add mushrooms and sauté until tender. Season with salt and pepper.
3. Lay two tortillas on a flat surface. Divide spinach, mushrooms, vegan cheese, and red onion evenly on the tortillas.
4. Place the remaining two tortillas on top of the filling, creating two quesadillas.
5. Place the quesadillas in the air fryer basket. Cook for 5 minutes, then flip and cook for an additional 5 minutes, or until the tortillas are golden and crispy.
6. Remove from the air fryer and let cool for a minute before slicing into wedges.
7. Serve hot and enjoy!

Nutrition Information (per serving): 350 Calories, 18g Fat, 34g Carbohydrates, 12g Protein, 4g Fiber

Sausage Patties

★★☆☆☆

COOK TIME: 12 MINUTES

PREP TIME: 10 MINUTES

SERVINGS: 4

INGREDIENTS

- 1 cup textured vegetable protein (TVP)
- 1 cup water
- 2 tbsp olive oil
- 2 tbsp soy sauce
- 1 tbsp nutritional yeast
- 1 tsp fennel seeds
- 1 tsp dried thyme
- 1 tsp garlic powder
- 1 tsp onion powder
- 1/2 tsp paprika
- Salt and pepper, to taste

INSTRUCTIONS

1. In a bowl, mix together the TVP and water. Let sit for 5 minutes.
2. In a separate bowl, mix together the olive oil, soy sauce, nutritional yeast, fennel seeds, thyme, garlic powder, onion powder, paprika, salt and pepper.
3. Drain any excess water from the TVP and add the TVP to the bowl with the spice mixture. Mix until well combined.
4. Divide the mixture into 8 equal portions and form into patties.
5. Place the patties in the air fryer basket in a single layer.
6. Cook at 400°F for 10 minutes, flipping the patties halfway through cooking, until crispy and golden.
7. Serve hot with your favorite breakfast items.

Nutrition values per serving (2 patties): 150 Calories, 10g Fat, 5g Carbohydrates, 10g Protein, 2g Fiber.

Sandwiches with Veggie Bacon

★ ☆ ☆ ☆ ☆

COOK TIME: 15 MINUTES

PREP TIME: 5 MINUTES

SERVINGS: 2

INGREDIENTS

- 4 slices of bread
- 4 vegan bacon strips
- 4 lettuce leaves
- 2 tomato slices
- 2 tablespoons vegan mayonnaise
- Salt and pepper to taste

INSTRUCTIONS

1. Preheat the air fryer to 400°F (200°C).
2. Place the vegan bacon strips in the air fryer basket and cook for 6-8 minutes, or until crispy.
3. Remove the bacon from the air fryer and set aside.
4. Toast the bread slices in the air fryer for 2 minutes.
5. Spread vegan mayonnaise on one side of each bread slice.
6. Layer lettuce, tomato slices, and cooked bacon on two bread slices.
7. Season with salt and pepper to taste.
8. Top with the remaining bread slices.
9. Place the sandwiches in the air fryer and cook for 2-3 minutes, or until the bread is toasted and the filling is warm.
10. Remove from the air fryer, cut in half, and serve.

Nutrition Information (per serving): 300 Calories, 10g Fat, 45g Carbohydrates, 10g Protein, 5g Fiber.

Waffles with Fresh Fruit

★ ☆ ☆ ☆ ☆

COOK TIME: 10 MINUTES

PREP TIME: 10 MINUTES

SERVINGS: 4

INGREDIENTS

- 1 cup all-purpose flour
- 1 tbsp sugar
- 2 tsp baking powder
- 1/4 tsp salt
- 1 cup non-dairy milk
- 2 tbsp melted vegan butter
- 1 tsp vanilla extract
- Fresh fruit of your choice (e.g. strawberries, blueberries, banana)

INSTRUCTIONS

1. In a large bowl, whisk together the flour, sugar, baking powder, and salt.
2. In a separate bowl, mix together the non-dairy milk, melted vegan butter, and vanilla extract.
3. Pour the wet ingredients into the dry ingredients and stir until just combined.
4. Preheat your air fryer to 400°F.
5. Spoon the batter into the air fryer basket, leaving space between each waffle, as they will expand while cooking.
6. Cook the waffles for 8-10 minutes, or until golden brown.
7. Serve the waffles warm, topped with fresh fruit of your choice.

Nutrition Information (per serving): Calories: 260; Fat: 11g; Carbohydrates: 37g; Protein: 5g; Sodium: 380mg

Potatoes with Rosemary and Garlic

★ ★ ☆ ☆ ☆

COOK TIME: 25 MINUTES

PREP TIME: 10 MINUTES

SERVINGS: 4

INGREDIENTS

- 4 medium-sized potatoes, washed and cubed
- 2 tablespoons olive oil
- 2 cloves garlic, minced
- 1 tablespoon fresh rosemary leaves, chopped
- Salt and pepper to taste

INSTRUCTIONS

1. Preheat the air fryer to 400°F (200°C).
2. In a mixing bowl, combine the cubed potatoes, olive oil, minced garlic, chopped rosemary leaves, salt, and pepper. Toss until the potatoes are well coated.
3. Place the seasoned potatoes in the air fryer basket in a single layer.
4. Cook for 20-25 minutes, shaking the basket halfway through, until the potatoes are crispy and golden brown.
5. Remove from the air fryer and serve hot.

Nutrition Information (per serving): 180 Calories, 7g Fat, 27g Carbohydrates, 3g Protein, 4g Fiber.

Baked Oatmeal with Nuts and Dried Fruit

★★ ✰ ✰ ✰

COOK TIME: 30 MINUTES

PREP TIME: 10 MINUTES

SERVINGS: 6

INGREDIENTS

- 2 cups rolled oats
- 1/2 cup chopped nuts (such as almonds, walnuts, or pecans)
- 1/2 cup dried fruit (such as raisins, cranberries, or chopped dates)
- 2 tablespoons maple syrup
- 2 cups plant-based milk (such as almond, soy, or oat milk)
- 1 teaspoon vanilla extract
- 1/2 teaspoon ground cinnamon
- 1/4 teaspoon salt

INSTRUCTIONS

1. Preheat the air fryer to 350°F (175°C).
2. In a mixing bowl, combine the rolled oats, chopped nuts, dried fruit, maple syrup, plant-based milk, vanilla extract, ground cinnamon, and salt. Stir until well combined.
3. Pour the mixture into a greased air fryer-safe baking dish.
4. Place the baking dish in the air fryer basket and cook for 25-30 minutes, or until the oatmeal is set and golden brown on top.
5. Remove from the air fryer and let cool for a few minutes before serving.

Nutrition Information (per serving): 240 Calories, 10g Fat, 34g Carbohydrates, 6g Protein, 5g Fiber.

Stuffed Peppers with Quinoa and Black Beans

★ ★ ☆ ☆ ☆

COOK TIME: 25 MINUTES

PREP TIME: 20 MINUTES

SERVINGS: 4

INGREDIENTS

- 4 bell peppers (any color)
- 1 cup cooked quinoa
- 1 cup canned black beans, rinsed and drained
- 1/2 cup diced tomatoes
- 1/2 cup diced onion
- 1/2 cup corn kernels
- 2 cloves garlic, minced
- 1 teaspoon ground cumin
- 1/2 teaspoon chili powder
- Salt and pepper to taste
- Fresh cilantro, for garnish

INSTRUCTIONS

1. Preheat the air fryer to 375°F (190°C).
2. Cut the tops off the bell peppers and remove the seeds and membranes.
3. In a mixing bowl, combine the cooked quinoa, black beans, diced tomatoes, onion, corn kernels, minced garlic, ground cumin, chili powder, salt, and pepper. Stir well to combine.
4. Stuff each bell pepper with the quinoa and black bean mixture.
5. Place the stuffed peppers in the air fryer basket and cook for 20-25 minutes, or until the peppers are tender and slightly charred.
6. Remove from the air fryer and garnish with fresh cilantro before serving.

Nutrition Information (per serving): 230 Calories, 1g Fat, 47g Carbohydrates, 11g Protein, 11g Fiber.

Breakfast Casserole with Tofu and Vegetables

★★ ☆ ☆ ☆

COOK TIME: 40 MINUTES

PREP TIME: 15 MINUTES

SERVINGS: 6

INGREDIENTS

- 1 block firm tofu, drained and crumbled
- 1 red bell pepper, diced
- 1 green bell pepper, diced
- 1 small onion, diced
- 2 cloves garlic, minced
- 1 cup spinach, chopped
- 1 cup mushrooms, sliced
- 1/2 cup nutritional yeast
- 2 tablespoons soy sauce
- 1 teaspoon turmeric
- 1/2 teaspoon paprika
- Salt and pepper to taste
- Cooking spray

INSTRUCTIONS

1. Preheat the air fryer to 375°F (190°C).
2. In a large skillet, sauté the bell peppers, onion, and garlic over medium heat until softened.
3. Add the crumbled tofu, spinach, and mushrooms to the skillet. Cook for an additional 5 minutes, until the tofu is heated through and the spinach wilts.
4. In a bowl, mix together the nutritional yeast, soy sauce, turmeric, paprika, salt, and pepper. Pour the mixture over the tofu and vegetables, stirring well to coat everything.
5. Lightly spray a baking dish with cooking spray. Transfer the tofu and vegetable mixture to the baking dish, spreading it evenly.
6. Place the baking dish in the air fryer basket and cook for 30-35 minutes, or until the casserole is firm and golden brown on top.
7. Remove from the air fryer and let it cool slightly before serving.

Nutrition Information (per serving): 150 Calories, 4g Fat, 13g Carbohydrates, 15g Protein, 4g Fiber.

Tacos with Tofu Scramble and Salsa

★★☆☆☆

COOK TIME: 15 MINUTES

PREP TIME: 10 MINUTES

SERVINGS: 4

INGREDIENTS

- 1 block firm tofu, drained and crumbled
- 1 tablespoon olive oil
- 1/2 small onion, diced
- 1/2 red bell pepper, diced
- 2 cloves garlic, minced
- 1 teaspoon ground cumin
- 1/2 teaspoon turmeric
- Salt and pepper to taste
- 8 small tortillas
- Salsa, for serving
- Fresh cilantro, for garnish

INSTRUCTIONS

1. Heat the olive oil in a skillet over medium heat. Add the onion, bell pepper, and garlic. Sauté until the vegetables are softened.
2. Add the crumbled tofu, cumin, turmeric, salt, and pepper to the skillet. Cook for about 5 minutes, until the tofu is heated through and well-coated with the spices.
3. Warm the tortillas in the air fryer for a few seconds, until pliable.
4. Spoon the tofu scramble onto each tortilla. Top with salsa and garnish with fresh cilantro.
5. Serve the tacos immediately.

Nutrition Information (per serving): 220 Calories, 8g Fat, 24g Carbohydrates, 12g Protein, 4g Fiber.

Strata with Grilled Veggies

★ ★ ☆ ☆ ☆

COOK TIME: 30 MINUTES

PREP TIME: 15 MINUTES

SERVINGS: 6

INGREDIENTS

- 6 slices of bread, cubed
- 1 cup grilled vegetables (such as zucchini, bell peppers, and eggplant), chopped
- 1 cup cherry tomatoes, halved
- 1 cup spinach, chopped
- 1 cup plant-based cheese, grated
- 4-5 tablespoons nutritional yeast
- 1 1/2 cups plant-based milk
- 1/4 cup chickpea flour
- 2 tablespoons olive oil
- 1 teaspoon dried basil
- 1/2 teaspoon dried thyme
- Salt and pepper to taste

INSTRUCTIONS

1. Preheat your air fryer to 350°F (175°C).
2. In a large bowl, combine the bread cubes, grilled vegetables, cherry tomatoes, spinach, plant-based cheese, nutritional yeast, dried basil, dried thyme, salt, and pepper.
3. In a separate bowl, whisk together the plant-based milk, chickpea flour, and olive oil until well combined.
4. Pour the milk mixture over the bread and vegetables, and toss gently to coat everything evenly.
5. Transfer the mixture to an air fryer-safe baking dish and spread it out evenly.
6. Place the baking dish in the air fryer basket and cook for 25-30 minutes, or until the strata is golden brown and set in the center.
7. Remove from the air fryer and let it cool slightly before serving.

Nutrition Information (per serving): 220 Calories, 10g Fat, 25g Carbohydrates, 9g Protein, 5g Fiber.

Sweet Potato Waffles with Maple Syrup

★ ☆ ☆ ☆ ☆

COOK TIME: 15 MINUTES

PREP TIME: 10 MINUTES

SERVINGS: 4

INGREDIENTS

- 2 cups cooked sweet potatoes, mashed
- 1 cup all-purpose flour
- 1 tablespoon baking powder
- 1 tablespoon ground flaxseed mixed with 3 tablespoons water (flaxseed egg)
- 1 cup plant-based milk
- 2 tablespoons maple syrup
- 1 teaspoon vanilla extract
- 1/2 teaspoon cinnamon
- Pinch of salt
- Maple syrup, for serving

INSTRUCTIONS

1. Preheat your air fryer to 380°F (190°C).
2. In a large mixing bowl, combine the mashed sweet potatoes, all-purpose flour, baking powder, flaxseed egg, plant-based milk, maple syrup, vanilla extract, cinnamon, and salt. Mix well until smooth and well combined.
3. Lightly grease the waffle iron with oil or cooking spray.
4. Spoon the sweet potato batter onto the preheated waffle iron and spread it evenly.
5. Close the waffle iron and cook for about 5-7 minutes, or until the waffles are golden brown and crispy.
6. Remove the waffles from the waffle iron and repeat with the remaining batter.
7. Serve the sweet potato waffles with maple syrup and any other desired toppings.

Nutrition Information (per serving): 250 Calories, 2g Fat, 52g Carbohydrates, 5g Protein, 5g Fiber.

Bake with Tofu and Broccoli

★★ ☆ ☆ ☆

COOK TIME: 25 MINUTES

PREP TIME: 15 MINUTES

SERVINGS: 4

INGREDIENTS

- 1 block of firm tofu, pressed and cubed
- 2 cups broccoli florets
- 1 red bell pepper, sliced
- 1 tablespoon soy sauce
- 1 tablespoon maple syrup
- 1 tablespoon sesame oil
- 1 teaspoon minced garlic
- 1/2 teaspoon ground ginger
- Salt and pepper, to taste

INSTRUCTIONS

1. Preheat your air fryer to 380°F (190°C).
2. In a bowl, whisk together the soy sauce, maple syrup, sesame oil, minced garlic, ground ginger, salt, and pepper.
3. Add the tofu, broccoli florets, and red bell pepper to the bowl and toss until well coated in the marinade.
4. Place the marinated tofu and vegetables in the air fryer basket in a single layer.
5. Cook for 20-25 minutes, shaking the basket halfway through, until the tofu is crispy and the vegetables are tender.
6. Serve the air-baked tofu and broccoli with rice or noodles, if desired.

Nutrition Information (per serving): 180 Calories, 8g Fat, 11g Carbohydrates, 15g Protein, 4g Fiber.

Frittata with Spinach and Tomatoes

★★ ☆ ☆ ☆

COOK TIME: 25 MINUTES

PREP TIME: 15 MINUTES

SERVINGS: 4

INGREDIENTS

- 1 cup firm tofu, crumbled
- 1 cup spinach, chopped
- 1 cup cherry tomatoes, halved
- 1/4 cup nutritional yeast
- 2 tablespoons almond milk
- 1 tablespoon olive oil
- 1 teaspoon garlic powder
- 1/2 teaspoon turmeric
- Salt and pepper, to taste

INSTRUCTIONS

1. Preheat your air fryer to 380°F (190°C).
2. In a bowl, combine the crumbled tofu, chopped spinach, halved cherry tomatoes, nutritional yeast, almond milk, olive oil, garlic powder, turmeric, salt, and pepper. Mix well.
3. Pour the mixture into a greased air fryer-safe baking dish.
4. Place the baking dish in the air fryer basket and cook for 20-25 minutes, until the frittata is set and slightly golden on top.
5. Remove from the air fryer and let it cool for a few minutes before slicing and serving.

Nutrition Information (per serving): 140 Calories, 9g Fat, 8g Carbohydrates, 9g Protein, 3g Fiber.

French Toast Casserole with Cinnamon and Maple Syrup

★★☆☆☆

COOK TIME: 25 MINUTES

PREP TIME: 15 MINUTES

SERVINGS: 4

INGREDIENTS

- 8 slices of day-old bread, preferably French bread
- 1 cup almond milk
- 1/4 cup maple syrup
- 1 teaspoon vanilla extract
- 1 teaspoon ground cinnamon
- Vegan butter or coconut oil, for greasing the baking dish
- Maple syrup, for serving
- Fresh berries, for serving

INSTRUCTIONS

1. Preheat your air fryer to 360°F (180°C).
2. In a bowl, whisk together the almond milk, maple syrup, vanilla extract, and ground cinnamon.
3. Grease a baking dish with vegan butter or coconut oil.
4. Dip each slice of bread into the almond milk mixture, allowing it to soak for a few seconds on each side.
5. Place the soaked bread slices in the greased baking dish, layering them evenly.
6. Pour any remaining almond milk mixture over the bread slices.
7. Place the baking dish in the air fryer basket and cook for 20-25 minutes, until the French toast is golden and crispy.
8. Remove from the air fryer and let it cool for a few minutes before serving.
9. Serve the French toast casserole with maple syrup and fresh berries.

Nutrition Information (per serving): 250 Calories, 5g Fat, 45g Carbohydrates, 5g Protein, 3g Fiber.

Bowl with Tofu Scramble and Roasted Veggies

★★☆☆☆

COOK TIME: 25 MINUTES

PREP TIME: 15 MINUTES

SERVINGS: 2

INGREDIENTS

- 1 block of firm tofu, drained and crumbled
- 1 tablespoon nutritional yeast
- 1/2 teaspoon turmeric
- 1/2 teaspoon garlic powder
- Salt and pepper, to taste
- 2 cups mixed roasted vegetables (such as bell peppers, zucchini, and sweet potatoes)
- 2 cups cooked quinoa or brown rice
- Fresh spinach or mixed greens, for serving
- Avocado slices, for serving
- Salsa or hot sauce, for serving

INSTRUCTIONS

1. Preheat your air fryer to 375°F (190°C).
2. In a bowl, mix the crumbled tofu, nutritional yeast, turmeric, garlic powder, salt, and pepper.
3. Place the seasoned tofu in the air fryer basket and cook for 10-12 minutes, shaking the basket halfway through, until the tofu is crispy and golden.
4. Meanwhile, prepare the roasted vegetables by tossing them with olive oil, salt, and pepper, then roast them in the air fryer for 12-15 minutes until they are tender and slightly charred.
5. Divide the cooked quinoa or brown rice between two bowls.
6. Top with the crispy tofu, roasted vegetables, fresh spinach or mixed greens, and avocado slices.
7. Serve the air bowl with salsa or hot sauce for added flavor.

Nutrition Information (per serving): 350 Calories, 10g Fat, 50g Carbohydrates, 18g Protein, 10g Fiber.

CHAPTER 2

Snacks and Appetizers

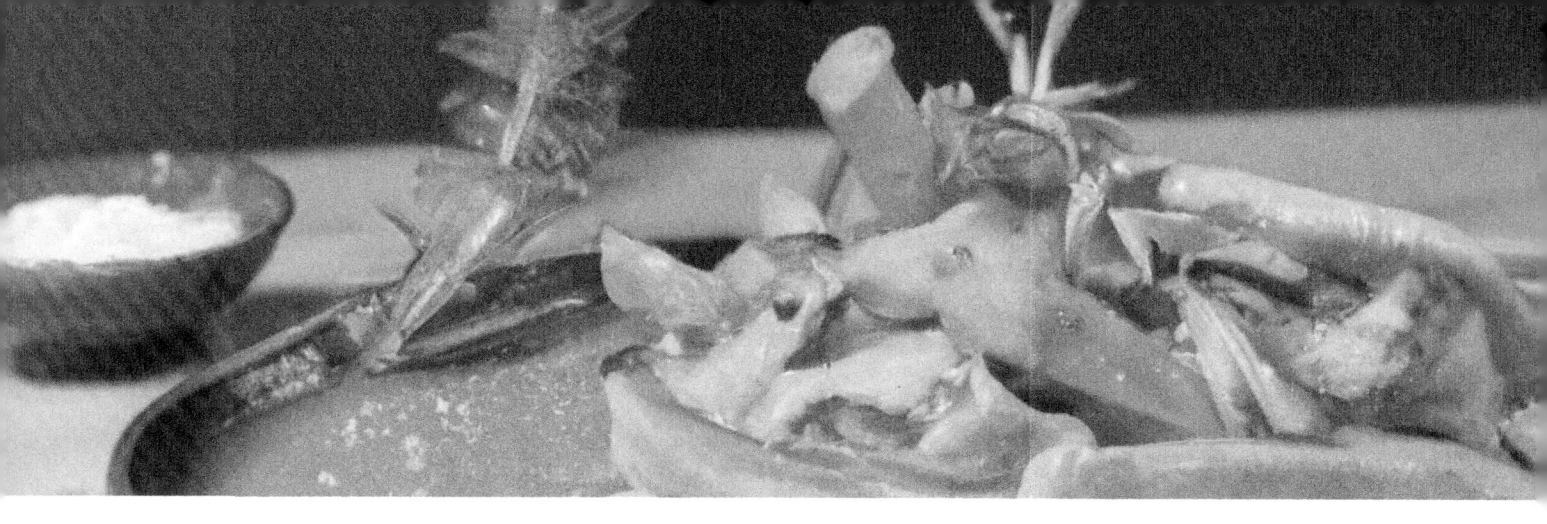

Sweet Potato Fries with Rosemary and Sea Salt

★★☆☆☆

COOK TIME: 20 MINUTES

PREP TIME: 10 MINUTES

SERVINGS: 4

INGREDIENTS

- 2 large sweet potatoes, peeled and cut into thin strips
- 2 tablespoons olive oil
- 1 tablespoon chopped fresh rosemary
- 1 teaspoon sea salt

INSTRUCTIONS

1. Preheat your air fryer to 400°F (200°C).
2. In a large bowl, toss the sweet potato strips with olive oil, rosemary, and sea salt until they are evenly coated.
3. Place the seasoned sweet potato strips in the air fryer basket in a single layer, working in batches if necessary.
4. Cook the sweet potato fries in the air fryer for 15-20 minutes, shaking the basket every 5 minutes to ensure even cooking, until they are crispy and golden brown.
5. Once cooked, remove the sweet potato fries from the air fryer and transfer them to a serving dish.
6. Serve the sweet potato fries immediately as a delicious and healthier alternative to traditional fries.

Nutrition Information (per serving): 180 Calories, 7g Fat, 28g Carbohydrates, 2g Protein, 4g Fiber.

Onion Rings with Spicy Dipping Sauce

★ ★ ★ ☆ ☆

COOK TIME: 15 MINUTES

PREP TIME: 20 MINUTES

SERVINGS: 4

INGREDIENTS

- 1/2 cup vegan mayonnaise
- 1 tablespoon ketchup
- 1 teaspoon hot sauce
- 1/2 teaspoon paprika
- 1/4 teaspoon garlic powder
- Salt and pepper to taste

INSTRUCTIONS

1. Preheat your air fryer to 400°F (200°C).
2. In a shallow bowl, mix together the flour, paprika, garlic powder, salt, and black pepper.
3. Dip the onion rings into the plant-based milk, then coat them with the flour mixture.
4. In another shallow bowl, place the bread crumbs.
5. Dip the coated onion rings into the bread crumbs, pressing gently to adhere.
6. Place the breaded onion rings in a single layer in the air fryer basket. You may need to work in batches.
7. Lightly spray the onion rings with cooking spray to help them brown.
8. Air fry the onion rings for about 10-15 minutes, or until golden brown and crispy, flipping them halfway through the cooking time.
9. Meanwhile, prepare the spicy dipping sauce by combining all the ingredients in a small bowl and stirring well.
10. Once the onion rings are cooked, transfer them to a serving plate and serve with the spicy dipping sauce.

Nutrition Information (per serving): 270 Calories, 10g Fat, 40g Carbohydrates, 4g Protein, 3g Fiber.

Zucchini Chips with Parmesan and Herbs

★★☆☆☆

COOK TIME: 12 MINUTES

PREP TIME: 15 MINUTES

SERVINGS: 4

INGREDIENTS

- 2 medium zucchini
- 1/2 cup bread crumbs
- 1/4 cup grated Parmesan cheese (vegan Parmesan for a vegan option)
- 1 teaspoon dried herbs (such as basil, oregano, or thyme)
- 1/2 teaspoon garlic powder
- 1/4 teaspoon salt
- 1/4 teaspoon black pepper
- Cooking spray

INSTRUCTIONS

1. Preheat your air fryer to 400°F (200°C).
2. Slice the zucchini into thin rounds, about 1/8 inch thick.
3. In a shallow bowl, combine the bread crumbs, grated Parmesan cheese, dried herbs, garlic powder, salt, and black pepper.
4. Dip each zucchini slice into the bread crumb mixture, pressing gently to adhere.
5. Place the breaded zucchini slices in a single layer in the air fryer basket. You may need to work in batches.
6. Lightly spray the zucchini slices with cooking spray to help them brown.
7. Air fry the zucchini chips for about 10-12 minutes, or until they are golden brown and crispy.
8. Once cooked, transfer the zucchini chips to a serving plate and let them cool slightly before serving.

Nutrition Information (per serving): 90 Calories, 3g Fat, 13g Carbohydrates, 5g Protein, 3g Fiber.

Falafel with Tahini Sauce

★★★☆☆

COOK TIME: 15 MINUTES

PREP TIME: 30 MINUTES

SERVINGS: 4

INGREDIENTS

- 1 can (15 ounces) chickpeas, drained and rinsed
- 1/2 small onion, chopped
- 2 garlic cloves, minced
- 2 tablespoons fresh parsley, chopped
- 2 tablespoons fresh cilantro, chopped
- 1 teaspoon ground cumin
- 1/2 teaspoon ground coriander
- 1/4 teaspoon cayenne pepper (optional, for spicier falafel)
- 2 tablespoons flour (all-purpose or chickpea flour for gluten-free)
- 1/2 teaspoon baking powder
- Salt and pepper, to taste
- Cooking spray

Tahini Sauce:

- 1/4 cup tahini
- 2 tablespoons lemon juice
- 2 tablespoons water
- 1 clove garlic, minced
- Salt, to taste

INSTRUCTIONS

1. In a food processor, combine the chickpeas, onion, garlic, parsley, cilantro, cumin, coriander, cayenne pepper (if using), flour, baking powder, salt, and pepper. Pulse until the mixture is well combined and forms a coarse paste.
2. Shape the mixture into small patties, about 1 inch in diameter.
3. Preheat your air fryer to 375°F (190°C).
4. Lightly spray the air fryer basket with cooking spray. Place the falafel patties in a single layer in the basket, without overcrowding.
5. Air fry the falafel for about 12-15 minutes, flipping them halfway through, until they are golden brown and crispy.
6. While the falafel is cooking, prepare the tahini sauce. In a small bowl, whisk together the tahini, lemon juice, water, minced garlic, and salt until smooth and well combined. Adjust the consistency by adding more water if needed.
7. Once the falafel is cooked, serve them warm with the tahini sauce for dipping or in pita bread with your favorite toppings.

Nutrition Information (per serving): 230 Calories, 10g Fat, 28g Carbohydrates, 9g Protein, 7g Fiber.

Carrot Fries with Curry Powder and Coconut Oil

★★☆☆☆

COOK TIME: 20 MINUTES

PREP TIME: 10 MINUTES

SERVINGS: 4

INGREDIENTS

- 4 large carrots, peeled and cut into thin strips
- 1 tablespoon coconut oil, melted
- 1 teaspoon curry powder
- 1/2 teaspoon salt
- Fresh cilantro, for garnish (optional)

INSTRUCTIONS

1. Preheat your air fryer to 400°F (200°C).
2. In a large bowl, combine the carrot strips, melted coconut oil, curry powder, and salt. Toss until the carrots are evenly coated with the oil and spices.
3. Place the coated carrot strips in a single layer in the air fryer basket. You may need to cook them in batches depending on the size of your air fryer.
4. Air fry the carrot fries for about 15-20 minutes, shaking the basket halfway through, until they are golden brown and crispy.
5. Once cooked, remove the carrot fries from the air fryer and garnish with fresh cilantro, if desired.
6. Serve the carrot fries immediately as a snack or as a side dish with your favorite dipping sauce.

Nutrition Information (per serving): 90 Calories, 4g Fat, 14g Carbohydrates, 1g Protein, 4g Fiber.

Spring Rolls with Sweet and Sour Sauce

★★☆☆☆

COOK TIME: 15 MINUTES

PREP TIME: 30 MINUTES

SERVINGS: 4

INGREDIENTS

For Spring Rolls:

- 8 spring roll wrappers
- 1 cup shredded cabbage
- 1 cup shredded carrots
- 1/2 cup bean sprouts
- 1/2 cup sliced bell peppers
- 1/2 cup sliced cucumber
- Fresh herbs like mint and cilantro, for garnish
- Rice vermicelli noodles, cooked according to package instructions

For Sweet and Sour Sauce:

- 1/4 cup rice vinegar
- 2 tablespoons soy sauce
- 2 tablespoons ketchup
- 2 tablespoons agave syrup or maple syrup
- 1 tablespoon cornstarch
- 1/4 cup water

INSTRUCTIONS

1. In a small bowl, whisk together all the ingredients for the sweet and sour sauce until well combined. Set aside.
2. Dip a spring roll wrapper into warm water for a few seconds until it softens. Place the wrapper on a clean surface.
3. Arrange a small portion of the shredded cabbage, carrots, bean sprouts, bell peppers, cucumber, and a few strands of cooked rice vermicelli noodles in the center of the wrapper.
4. Fold the sides of the wrapper over the filling, then roll it up tightly from the bottom to form a spring roll. Repeat with the remaining ingredients.
5. Preheat your air fryer to 375°F (190°C).
6. Place the spring rolls in a single layer in the air fryer basket, leaving space between each roll. Cook for about 8-10 minutes until they are golden and crispy.
7. Serve the air-fried spring rolls with the sweet and sour sauce on the side for dipping. Garnish with fresh herbs, if desired.

Nutrition Information (per serving): 200 Calories, 1g Fat, 46g Carbohydrates, 4g Protein, 4g Fiber.

Portobello Mushroom Caps with Balsamic Glaze

★ ★ ★ ☆ ☆

COOK TIME: 20 MINUTES

PREP TIME: 10 MINUTES

SERVINGS: 4

INGREDIENTS

- 4 large Portobello mushroom caps
- 2 tablespoons olive oil
- 2 tablespoons balsamic vinegar
- 2 cloves garlic, minced
- 1/2 teaspoon dried thyme
- Salt and pepper, to taste
- Fresh parsley, for garnish

INSTRUCTIONS

1. Preheat your air fryer to 375°F (190°C).
2. In a small bowl, whisk together olive oil, balsamic vinegar, minced garlic, dried thyme, salt, and pepper.
3. Brush the marinade onto both sides of the Portobello mushroom caps.
4. Place the mushroom caps in the air fryer basket, gill-side down.
5. Cook for about 15-20 minutes, or until the mushrooms are tender and slightly browned, flipping halfway through the cooking time.
6. Remove the mushroom caps from the air fryer and garnish with fresh parsley.
7. Serve the Portobello mushroom caps as a side dish or as a burger alternative.

Nutrition Information (per serving): 80 Calories, 6g Fat, 6g Carbohydrates, 2g Protein, 2g Fiber.

Tofu Bites with Buffalo Sauce and Ranch Dipping Sauce

★★☆☆☆

COOK TIME: 20 MINUTES

PREP TIME: 15 MINUTES

SERVINGS: 4

INGREDIENTS

- 1 block firm tofu, pressed and drained
- 1/4 cup all-purpose flour
- 1/4 cup cornstarch
- 1/2 teaspoon garlic powder
- 1/2 teaspoon onion powder
- 1/4 teaspoon paprika
- 1/4 teaspoon salt
- 1/4 teaspoon black pepper
- 1/2 cup buffalo sauce
- Ranch dressing, for dipping

INSTRUCTIONS

1. Preheat your air fryer to 400°F (200°C).
2. Cut the tofu into bite-sized cubes.
3. In a shallow bowl, mix together flour, cornstarch, garlic powder, onion powder, paprika, salt, and black pepper.
4. Coat each tofu cube with the flour mixture, shaking off any excess.
5. Place the coated tofu cubes in the air fryer basket in a single layer.
6. Air fry for 10 minutes, flipping the tofu halfway through the cooking time.
7. Remove the tofu from the air fryer and transfer it to a bowl. Pour the buffalo sauce over the tofu and toss to coat evenly.
8. Return the coated tofu to the air fryer basket and air fry for another 5 minutes.
9. Serve the tofu bites with ranch dressing for dipping.

Nutrition Information (per serving): 180 Calories, 6g Fat, 19g Carbohydrates, 11g Protein, 2g Fiber.

Brussels Sprouts with Balsamic Vinegar and Honey

★★★☆☆

COOK TIME: 20 MINUTES

PREP TIME: 10 MINUTES

SERVINGS: 4

INGREDIENTS

- 1 pound Brussels sprouts, trimmed and halved
- 2 tablespoons olive oil
- 2 tablespoons balsamic vinegar
- 1 tablespoon honey (or maple syrup for vegan option)
- Salt and pepper, to taste

INSTRUCTIONS

1. Preheat your air fryer to 400°F (200°C).
2. In a bowl, toss the Brussels sprouts with olive oil, balsamic vinegar, honey (or maple syrup), salt, and pepper until well coated.
3. Place the coated Brussels sprouts in the air fryer basket in a single layer.
4. Air fry for 15-20 minutes, shaking the basket halfway through the cooking time, until the Brussels sprouts are tender and crispy.
5. Remove from the air fryer and serve hot.

Nutrition Information (per serving): 120 Calories, 6g Fat, 16g Carbohydrates, 4g Protein, 4g Fiber.

Cauliflower Wings with Barbecue Sauce

★★☆☆☆

COOK TIME: 25 MINUTES

PREP TIME: 15 MINUTES

SERVINGS: 4

INGREDIENTS

- 1 large head of cauliflower, cut into florets
- 1 cup breadcrumbs (use gluten-free breadcrumbs for a gluten-free version)
- 1 teaspoon smoked paprika
- 1/2 teaspoon garlic powder
- 1/2 teaspoon onion powder
- 1/4 teaspoon salt
- 1/4 teaspoon black pepper
- 1/2 cup barbecue sauce (use a vegan barbecue sauce for a vegan version)
- Cooking spray

INSTRUCTIONS

1. Preheat your air fryer to 400°F (200°C).
2. In a large bowl, combine the breadcrumbs, smoked paprika, garlic powder, onion powder, salt, and black pepper.
3. Dip each cauliflower floret into the barbecue sauce, then roll it in the breadcrumb mixture until coated evenly.
4. Place the coated cauliflower florets in a single layer in the air fryer basket. You may need to cook them in batches depending on the size of your air fryer.
5. Lightly spray the cauliflower with cooking spray.
6. Air fry for 20-25 minutes, or until the cauliflower is crispy and golden brown, flipping them halfway through the cooking time.
7. Serve the cauliflower wings hot with extra barbecue sauce for dipping.

Nutrition Information (per serving): 180 Calories, 2g Fat, 38g Carbohydrates, 5g Protein, 6g Fiber.

Sweet and Spicy Peppers with Vinegar and Honey

★★☆☆☆

COOK TIME: 15 MINUTES

PREP TIME: 10 MINUTES

SERVINGS: 4

INGREDIENTS

- 4 bell peppers (red, yellow, or orange), sliced
- 2 tablespoons olive oil
- 2 tablespoons apple cider vinegar
- 2 tablespoons honey (use agave syrup for a vegan version)
- 1 teaspoon chili flakes
- Salt to taste

INSTRUCTIONS

1. Preheat your air fryer to 400°F (200°C).
2. In a bowl, combine the olive oil, apple cider vinegar, honey (or agave syrup), chili flakes, and salt. Mix well.
3. Add the sliced bell peppers to the bowl and toss them in the marinade until they are well coated.
4. Place the marinated bell peppers in the air fryer basket in a single layer.
5. Air fry for 12-15 minutes, or until the peppers are tender and slightly charred, stirring halfway through the cooking time.
6. Serve the sweet and spicy peppers as a side dish or as a topping for sandwiches, tacos, or salads.

Nutrition Information (per serving): 90 Calories, 5g Fat, 12g Carbohydrates, 1g Protein, 3g Fiber.

Artichoke Hearts with Lemon and Garlic

★★★☆☆

COOK TIME: 15 MINUTES

PREP TIME: 10 MINUTES

SERVINGS: 4

INGREDIENTS

- 1 can artichoke hearts, drained and quartered
- 2 tablespoons olive oil
- 2 cloves garlic, minced
- Juice of 1 lemon
- Salt and pepper to taste

INSTRUCTIONS

1. Preheat your air fryer to 400°F (200°C).
2. In a bowl, combine the olive oil, minced garlic, lemon juice, salt, and pepper.
3. Add the quartered artichoke hearts to the bowl and toss them in the marinade until they are well coated.
4. Place the marinated artichoke hearts in the air fryer basket in a single layer.
5. Air fry for 12-15 minutes, or until the artichoke hearts are golden brown and crispy, shaking the basket halfway through the cooking time.
6. Serve the air-fried artichoke hearts as a delicious appetizer or side dish.

Nutrition Information (per serving): 120 Calories, 9g Fat, 10g Carbohydrates, 2g Protein, 4g Fiber.

Spiced Chickpeas with Cumin and Paprika

★ ☆ ☆ ☆ ☆

COOK TIME: 15 MINUTES

PREP TIME: 5 MINUTES

SERVINGS: 4

INGREDIENTS

- 1 can chickpeas, drained and rinsed
- 1 tablespoon olive oil
- 1 teaspoon ground cumin
- 1 teaspoon paprika
- 1/2 teaspoon salt
- 1/4 teaspoon black pepper

INSTRUCTIONS

1. Preheat your air fryer to 400°F (200°C).
2. In a bowl, combine the chickpeas, olive oil, cumin, paprika, salt, and black pepper. Toss to coat the chickpeas evenly.
3. Place the seasoned chickpeas in the air fryer basket in a single layer.
4. Air fry for 12-15 minutes, shaking the basket halfway through the cooking time, until the chickpeas are crispy and golden brown.
5. Remove the chickpeas from the air fryer and let them cool slightly before serving.

Nutrition Information (per serving): 150 Calories, 5g Fat, 20g Carbohydrates, 6g Protein, 6g Fiber.

Stuffed Jalapenos with Cream Cheese and Chives

★ ★ ★ ☆ ☆

COOK TIME:
12 MINUTES

PREP TIME:
15 MINUTES

SERVINGS:
4

INGREDIENTS

- 8 jalapeno peppers
- 4 ounces cream cheese, softened
- 2 tablespoons chopped chives
- Salt and pepper to taste
- 1/2 cup breadcrumbs

INSTRUCTIONS

1. Preheat your air fryer to 375°F (190°C).
2. Cut each jalapeno pepper in half lengthwise and remove the seeds and membranes.
3. In a bowl, mix together the softened cream cheese, chopped chives, salt, and pepper.
4. Spoon the cream cheese mixture into each jalapeno half and press the two halves back together.
5. Roll each stuffed jalapeno in breadcrumbs, pressing gently to adhere.
6. Place the stuffed jalapenos in the air fryer basket in a single layer.
7. Air fry for 10-12 minutes until the jalapenos are tender and the breadcrumbs are golden brown.
8. Remove from the air fryer and let them cool slightly before serving.

Nutrition Information (per serving): 130 Calories, 9g Fat, 10g Carbohydrates, 4g Protein, 1g Fiber.

Baked Sweet Potato Rounds with Cinnamon and Maple Syrup

★ ★ ☆ ☆ ☆

COOK TIME: 20 MINUTES

PREP TIME: 10 MINUTES

SERVINGS: 4

INGREDIENTS

- 2 large sweet potatoes, sliced into rounds
- 2 tablespoons olive oil
- 1 teaspoon cinnamon
- 2 tablespoons maple syrup
- Salt to taste

INSTRUCTIONS

1. Preheat your air fryer to 400°F (200°C).
2. In a bowl, toss the sweet potato rounds with olive oil, cinnamon, and salt until well coated.
3. Place the sweet potato rounds in a single layer in the air fryer basket.
4. Air fry for 10 minutes, then flip the rounds over and air fry for another 10 minutes, or until they are crispy and golden brown.
5. Remove the sweet potato rounds from the air fryer and drizzle them with maple syrup.
6. Toss the rounds gently to evenly coat them with the syrup.
7. Serve hot as a snack or side dish.

Nutrition Information (per serving): 160 Calories, 5g Fat, 28g Carbohydrates, 2g Protein, 4g Fiber.

Eggplant Parmesan Bites with Marinara Sauce and Vegan Cheese

★★★★☆

COOK TIME:
20 MINUTES

PREP TIME:
15 MINUTES

SERVINGS:
4

INGREDIENTS

- 1 medium eggplant
- 1 cup breadcrumbs (can use gluten-free breadcrumbs if desired)
- 1 teaspoon dried Italian seasoning
- 1/2 teaspoon garlic powder
- 1/2 teaspoon onion powder
- Salt and pepper to taste
- 1/4 cup all-purpose flour (or gluten-free flour)
- 1/2 cup non-dairy milk (such as almond milk or soy milk)
- 1 cup marinara sauce
- 1/2 cup vegan cheese, shredded (such as vegan mozzarella or cheddar)

INSTRUCTIONS

1. Preheat your air fryer to 375°F (190°C).
2. Slice the eggplant into 1/2-inch thick rounds.
3. In a shallow bowl, combine the breadcrumbs, dried Italian seasoning, garlic powder, onion powder, salt, and pepper.
4. Place the flour and non-dairy milk in separate bowls.
5. Dip each eggplant round into the flour, then into the non-dairy milk, and finally into the breadcrumb mixture, ensuring it is well coated.
6. Place the coated eggplant rounds in a single layer in the air fryer basket.
7. Air fry for 10 minutes, flip the rounds over, and air fry for another 5-7 minutes, or until they are crispy and golden brown.
8. Remove the eggplant rounds from the air fryer and top each round with a spoonful of marinara sauce and a sprinkle of vegan cheese.
9. Return the eggplant rounds to the air fryer and air fry for an additional 2-3 minutes, or until the cheese is melted.
10. Serve hot with extra marinara sauce on the side for dipping.

Nutrition Information (per serving): 230 Calories, 5g Fat, 39g Carbohydrates, 8g Protein, 7g Fiber.

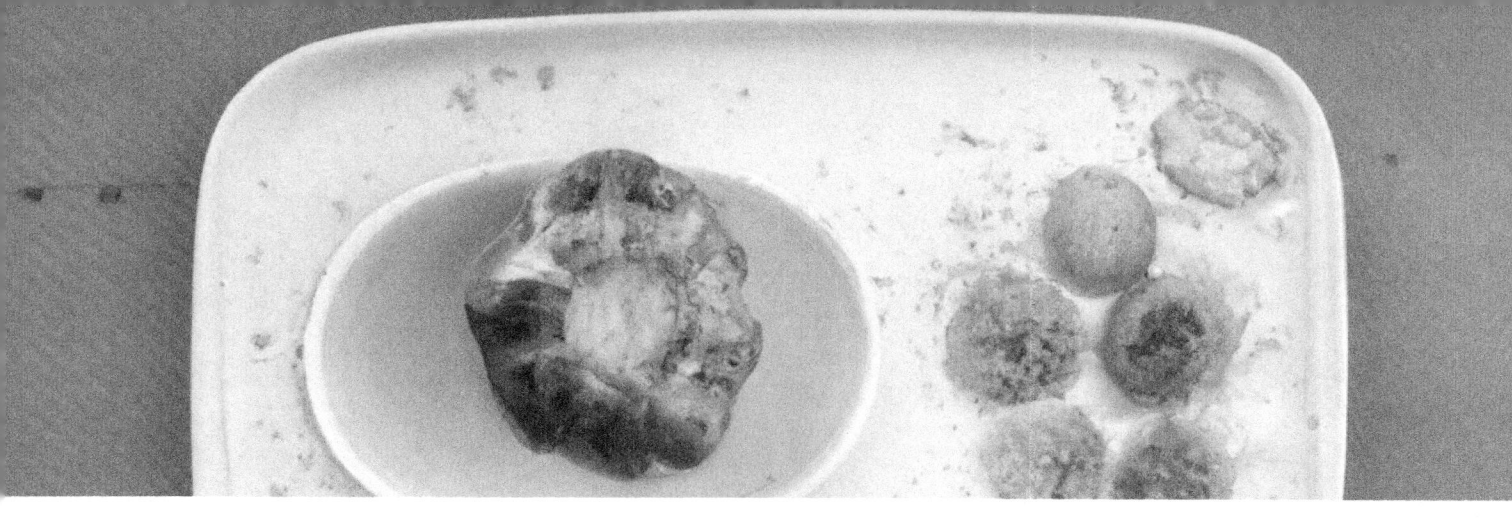

Roasted Garlic with Olive Oil and Sea Salt

★ ★ ☆ ☆ ☆

COOK TIME: 30 MINUTES

PREP TIME: 5 MINUTES

SERVINGS: 4

INGREDIENTS

- 4 whole garlic bulbs
- 2 tablespoons olive oil
- Sea salt, to taste

INSTRUCTIONS

1. Preheat your air fryer to 400°F (200°C).
2. Peel away the outer layers of the garlic bulbs, leaving the individual cloves intact.
3. Cut off the top of each garlic bulb to expose the cloves.
4. Place the garlic bulbs in the center of a piece of aluminum foil.
5. Drizzle the olive oil over the garlic bulbs, ensuring they are well coated.
6. Sprinkle sea salt over the garlic bulbs.
7. Fold the foil over the garlic bulbs to create a packet, ensuring it is tightly sealed.
8. Place the foil packet in the air fryer basket.
9. Air fry for 25-30 minutes, or until the garlic cloves are soft and golden brown.
10. Remove the foil packet from the air fryer and let it cool for a few minutes.
11. Once cooled, squeeze the roasted garlic cloves out of their skins.

Nutrition Information (per serving): 60 Calories, 4g Fat, 5g Carbohydrates, 1g Protein, 0g Fiber.

Fried Rice Balls with Vegetables and Tamari

★★★★☆

COOK TIME: 15 MINUTES

PREP TIME: 20 MINUTES

SERVINGS: 4

INGREDIENTS

- 2 cups cooked rice (preferably day-old)
- 1 cup mixed vegetables (such as carrots, peas, and corn), diced
- 2 tablespoons tamari (or soy sauce)
- 1 teaspoon sesame oil
- 1/2 teaspoon garlic powder
- 1/4 teaspoon onion powder
- 1/4 teaspoon ginger powder
- 1/4 teaspoon black pepper
- 1/4 cup all-purpose flour
- 1/4 cup water
- 1 cup panko breadcrumbs
- Cooking spray

INSTRUCTIONS

1. In a large mixing bowl, combine the cooked rice, diced vegetables, tamari, sesame oil, garlic powder, onion powder, ginger powder, and black pepper. Mix well until all ingredients are evenly combined.
2. In a small bowl, mix the flour and water together to create a thick paste.
3. Take a small handful of the rice mixture and shape it into a ball. Dip the ball into the flour paste, ensuring it is well coated.
4. Roll the ball in panko breadcrumbs until it is completely covered. Repeat this process with the remaining rice mixture.
5. Preheat your air fryer to 400°F (200°C).
6. Lightly coat the air fryer basket with cooking spray.
7. Place the coated rice balls in a single layer in the air fryer basket, without overcrowding.
8. Spray the tops of the rice balls with cooking spray.
9. Air fry for 10-12 minutes, flipping halfway through, or until the rice balls are golden brown and crispy.
10. Serve the air fryer fried rice balls hot with your favorite dipping sauce.

Nutrition Information (per serving): 180 Calories, 2g Fat, 37g Carbohydrates, 4g Protein, 2g Fiber.

Spiced Nuts with Cayenne and Maple Syrup

★★☆☆☆

COOK TIME: 15 MINUTES

PREP TIME: 5 MINUTES

SERVINGS: 4

INGREDIENTS

- 2 cups mixed nuts (such as almonds, cashews, and walnuts)
- 2 tablespoons maple syrup
- 1 teaspoon ground cayenne pepper
- 1/2 teaspoon ground cinnamon
- 1/2 teaspoon salt

INSTRUCTIONS

1. Preheat your air fryer to 350°F (175°C).
2. In a bowl, mix together the maple syrup, cayenne pepper, cinnamon, and salt.
3. Add the mixed nuts to the bowl and toss to coat them evenly with the spiced maple syrup mixture.
4. Transfer the coated nuts to the air fryer basket, spreading them out in a single layer.
5. Air fry for 10 minutes, shaking the basket halfway through to ensure even cooking.
6. Remove the nuts from the air fryer and let them cool completely before serving.

Nutrition Information (per serving): 240 Calories, 20g Fat, 10g Carbohydrates, 6g Protein, 3g Fiber.

Baked Mac and Cheese Bites with Panko Breadcrumbs

★★☆☆☆

COOK TIME: 12 MINUTES

PREP TIME: 20 MINUTES

SERVINGS: 4

INGREDIENTS

- 2 cups cooked macaroni
- 1 cup shredded cheddar cheese
- 1/4 cup grated Parmesan cheese
- 1/4 cup milk
- 1/4 cup breadcrumbs (preferably panko)
- 1/2 teaspoon garlic powder
- 1/2 teaspoon onion powder
- 1/4 teaspoon salt
- 1/4 teaspoon black pepper
- Cooking spray

INSTRUCTIONS

1. In a large bowl, combine the cooked macaroni, cheddar cheese, Parmesan cheese, milk, garlic powder, onion powder, salt, and black pepper. Mix well until everything is evenly combined.
2. Using your hands, shape the mixture into bite-sized balls.
3. Place the breadcrumbs in a shallow dish. Roll each mac and cheese ball in the breadcrumbs, pressing lightly to adhere.
4. Preheat your air fryer to 375°F (190°C).
5. Lightly spray the air fryer basket with cooking spray. Place the mac and cheese bites in the basket in a single layer, without overcrowding.
6. Air fry for 10-12 minutes, or until the bites are golden and crispy on the outside.
7. Serve the mac and cheese bites hot, with your favorite dipping sauce if desired.

Nutrition Information (per serving): 280 Calories, 12g Fat, 29g Carbohydrates, 13g Protein, 2g Fiber.

Chapter 3

Main Dishes

Tofu and Vegetable Stir-Fry with Sesame Oil and Soy Sauce

★★☆☆☆

COOK TIME: 20 MINUTES

PREP TIME: 15 MINUTES

SERVINGS: 4

INGREDIENTS

- 1 block of tofu, pressed and cubed
- 2 cups mixed vegetables (such as bell peppers, broccoli, carrots, and snap peas), sliced
- 2 tablespoons sesame oil
- 2 tablespoons soy sauce
- 1 tablespoon cornstarch
- 1 tablespoon water
- 1 teaspoon minced garlic
- 1 teaspoon grated ginger
- 1/2 teaspoon red pepper flakes (optional)
- Salt, to taste
- Cooking spray

INSTRUCTIONS

1. In a small bowl, whisk together the cornstarch and water to make a slurry. Set aside.
2. In a large mixing bowl, combine the cubed tofu, sliced vegetables, sesame oil, soy sauce, minced garlic, grated ginger, red pepper flakes (if using), and salt. Toss everything together until well-coated.
3. Preheat your air fryer to 400°F (200°C).
4. Lightly spray the air fryer basket with cooking spray. Place the tofu and vegetable mixture in the basket in a single layer, without overcrowding.
5. Air fry for 15-20 minutes, shaking the basket every 5 minutes to ensure even cooking. The tofu should be golden and the vegetables should be crisp-tender.
6. Once done, drizzle the cornstarch slurry over the tofu and vegetables. Toss gently to coat and cook for an additional 1-2 minutes to thicken the sauce.
7. Serve the stir-fry hot, over cooked rice or noodles if desired.

Nutrition Information (per serving): 220 Calories, 12g Fat, 14g Carbohydrates, 16g Protein, 4g Fiber.

Sweet Potato and Black Bean Tacos with Avocado Cream Sauce

★★★☆☆

COOK TIME: 20 MINUTES

PREP TIME: 15 MINUTES

SERVINGS: 4

INGREDIENTS

- 2 medium sweet potatoes, peeled and diced
- 1 can black beans, rinsed and drained
- 1 teaspoon cumin
- 1 teaspoon chili powder
- 1/2 teaspoon garlic powder
- Salt, to taste
- 8 small corn tortillas
- Cooking spray

For the Avocado Cream Sauce:

- 1 ripe avocado
- 1/4 cup plain Greek yogurt (or dairy-free alternative for vegan version)
- 1 tablespoon lime juice
- 1 clove garlic, minced
- Salt, to taste

Optional toppings:

- Chopped fresh cilantro
- Diced red onion
- Sliced jalapenos
- Lime wedges

INSTRUCTIONS

1. Preheat your air fryer to 400°F (200°C).
2. In a mixing bowl, combine the diced sweet potatoes, cumin, chili powder, garlic powder, and salt. Toss to coat the sweet potatoes evenly with the spices.
3. Lightly spray the air fryer basket with cooking spray. Place the seasoned sweet potatoes in the basket in a single layer, without overcrowding.
4. Air fry for 15-20 minutes, shaking the basket halfway through cooking, until the sweet potatoes are tender and slightly crispy.
5. While the sweet potatoes are cooking, prepare the avocado cream sauce. In a blender or food processor, combine the avocado, Greek yogurt, lime juice, minced garlic, and salt. Blend until smooth and creamy. Adjust the seasoning if needed.
6. Warm the corn tortillas in a dry skillet or microwave until soft and pliable.
7. Assemble the tacos by spreading a spoonful of avocado cream sauce onto each tortilla. Top with a scoop of black beans and a generous amount of air-fried sweet potatoes. Add any desired toppings, such as chopped cilantro, diced red onion, sliced jalapenos, and a squeeze of lime juice.
8. Serve the sweet potato and black bean tacos immediately.

Nutrition Information (per serving): 280 Calories, 5g Fat, 52g Carbohydrates, 9g Protein, 12g Fiber.

Chickpea Curry with Coconut Milk and Spices

★ ★ ☆ ☆ ☆

COOK TIME: 25 MINUTES

PREP TIME: 10 MINUTES

SERVINGS: 4

INGREDIENTS

- 2 cans chickpeas, rinsed and drained
- 1 onion, diced
- 2 cloves garlic, minced
- 1 red bell pepper, diced
- 1 can coconut milk
- 2 tablespoons curry powder
- 1 teaspoon ground cumin
- 1 teaspoon ground coriander
- 1/2 teaspoon turmeric
- Salt and pepper, to taste
- Fresh cilantro, for garnish

INSTRUCTIONS

1. Preheat your air fryer to 400°F (200°C).
2. In a large bowl, combine the chickpeas, onion, garlic, red bell pepper, coconut milk, curry powder, cumin, coriander, turmeric, salt, and pepper. Mix well to ensure all ingredients are coated in the spices.
3. Transfer the chickpea mixture to the air fryer basket in a single layer, without overcrowding.
4. Air fry for 20-25 minutes, shaking the basket occasionally, until the chickpeas are crispy and golden brown.
5. Serve the air-fried chickpea curry over rice or with naan bread. Garnish with fresh cilantro.

Nutrition Information (per serving): 380 Calories, 17g Fat, 46g Carbohydrates, 12g Protein, 12g Fiber.

Quinoa and Vegetable Bowl with Lemon and Olive Oil

★★★☆☆

COOK TIME: 15 MINUTES

PREP TIME: 10 MINUTES

SERVINGS: 4

INGREDIENTS

- 1 cup quinoa, rinsed
- 2 cups vegetable broth
- 1 bell pepper, diced
- 1 zucchini, diced
- 1 cup cherry tomatoes, halved
- 1/4 cup red onion, diced
- 2 tablespoons olive oil
- Juice of 1 lemon
- Salt and pepper, to taste
- Fresh parsley, for garnish

INSTRUCTIONS

1. Preheat your air fryer to 400°F (200°C).
2. In a saucepan, combine the quinoa and vegetable broth. Bring to a boil, then reduce heat and simmer for about 15 minutes, or until the quinoa is cooked and the liquid is absorbed.
3. In a mixing bowl, combine the cooked quinoa, bell pepper, zucchini, cherry tomatoes, red onion, olive oil, lemon juice, salt, and pepper. Toss well to coat all the ingredients.
4. Transfer the quinoa and vegetable mixture to the air fryer basket in a single layer, without overcrowding.
5. Air fry for 8-10 minutes, shaking the basket occasionally, until the vegetables are tender and slightly charred.
6. Serve the air-fried quinoa and vegetable bowl as a main dish or side dish. Garnish with fresh parsley.

Nutrition Information (per serving): 240 Calories, 9g Fat, 32g Carbohydrates, 7g Protein, 6g Fiber.

Ratatouille with Tomato Sauce and Herbs

★★★★★

COOK TIME: 20 MINUTES

PREP TIME: 15 MINUTES

SERVINGS: 4

INGREDIENTS

- 1 eggplant, diced
- 1 zucchini, diced
- 1 yellow squash, diced
- 1 red bell pepper, diced
- 1 yellow bell pepper, diced
- 1 onion, diced
- 3 cloves garlic, minced
- 2 cups tomato sauce
- 2 tablespoons olive oil
- 1 teaspoon dried thyme
- 1 teaspoon dried basil
- 1 teaspoon dried oregano
- Salt and pepper, to taste
- Fresh parsley, for garnish

INSTRUCTIONS

1. Preheat your air fryer to 375°F (190°C).
2. In a large bowl, combine the diced eggplant, zucchini, yellow squash, bell peppers, onion, garlic, olive oil, dried thyme, dried basil, dried oregano, salt, and pepper. Toss well to coat the vegetables evenly.
3. Transfer the vegetable mixture to the air fryer basket, spreading it out in an even layer.
4. Air fry for 15-20 minutes, shaking the basket once or twice during cooking, until the vegetables are tender and slightly charred.
5. In a separate saucepan, heat the tomato sauce over medium heat until warmed through.
6. Once the vegetables are done, transfer them to a serving dish and pour the tomato sauce over them. Mix well to combine.
7. Garnish with fresh parsley and serve the air-fried ratatouille as a main dish or side dish.

Nutrition Information (per serving): 180 Calories, 7g Fat, 27g Carbohydrates, 5g Protein, 8g Fiber.

Roasted Vegetable and Rice Casserole with Vegan Cheese

★ ★ ★ ☆ ☆

COOK TIME: 35 MINUTES

PREP TIME: 20 MINUTES

SERVINGS: 4

INGREDIENTS

- 2 cups cooked rice
- 1 small head cauliflower, cut into florets
- 2 cups broccoli florets
- 1 red bell pepper, sliced
- 1 yellow bell pepper, sliced
- 1 zucchini, sliced
- 1 onion, sliced
- 2 tablespoons olive oil
- 1 teaspoon garlic powder
- 1 teaspoon onion powder
- 1 teaspoon paprika
- Salt and pepper, to taste
- 1 cup vegan cheese, shredded

INSTRUCTIONS

1. Preheat your air fryer to 400°F (200°C).
2. In a large bowl, combine the cauliflower florets, broccoli florets, bell peppers, zucchini, onion, olive oil, garlic powder, onion powder, paprika, salt, and pepper. Toss well to coat the vegetables evenly.
3. Transfer the vegetable mixture to the air fryer basket, spreading it out in an even layer.
4. Air fry for 15-20 minutes, shaking the basket once or twice during cooking, until the vegetables are tender and slightly charred.
5. In a greased casserole dish, layer the cooked rice and roasted vegetables. Sprinkle the vegan cheese on top.
6. Place the casserole dish in the air fryer and cook for an additional 10-15 minutes, until the cheese is melted and bubbly.
7. Serve the air-fried roasted vegetable and rice casserole hot as a main dish or side dish.

Nutrition Information (per serving): 300 Calories, 12g Fat, 40g Carbohydrates, 8g Protein, 8g Fiber.

Teriyaki Tofu and Vegetables with Rice

★★☆☆☆

COOK TIME: 20 MINUTES

PREP TIME: 30 MINUTES

SERVINGS: 4

INGREDIENTS

- 14 ounces firm tofu, drained and cubed
- 2 cups mixed vegetables (such as broccoli, bell peppers, carrots)
- 1/4 cup teriyaki sauce
- 1 tablespoon soy sauce
- 1 tablespoon rice vinegar
- 1 tablespoon honey or maple syrup (for vegan version, use maple syrup)
- 1 teaspoon minced garlic
- 1 teaspoon grated ginger
- 2 cups cooked rice
- Sesame seeds, for garnish (optional)
- Green onions, chopped, for garnish (optional)

INSTRUCTIONS

1. Preheat your air fryer to 400°F (200°C).
2. In a bowl, combine teriyaki sauce, soy sauce, rice vinegar, honey or maple syrup, minced garlic, and grated ginger. Stir well to combine.
3. Place the tofu cubes in a shallow dish and pour half of the teriyaki sauce mixture over the tofu. Allow it to marinate for 15 minutes.
4. Place the marinated tofu in the air fryer basket and cook for 10 minutes, flipping halfway through.
5. In another bowl, toss the mixed vegetables with the remaining teriyaki sauce mixture.
6. After 10 minutes, add the vegetables to the air fryer basket with the tofu and cook for an additional 8-10 minutes, until the vegetables are tender-crisp.
7. Serve the air-fried teriyaki tofu and vegetables over cooked rice. Garnish with sesame seeds and chopped green onions, if desired.

Nutrition Information (per serving): 320 Calories, 6g Fat, 54g Carbohydrates, 15g Protein, 6g Fiber.

Cauliflower Steaks with Romesco Sauce and Almonds

★★☆☆☆

COOK TIME: 20 MINUTES

PREP TIME: 10 MINUTES

SERVINGS: 2

INGREDIENTS

- 1 large head of cauliflower
- 2 tablespoons olive oil
- 1/2 teaspoon garlic powder
- 1/2 teaspoon smoked paprika
- Salt and pepper, to taste
- 1/4 cup sliced almonds, toasted
- Fresh parsley, chopped, for garnish (optional)

For the Romesco Sauce:
- 1/2 cup roasted red bell peppers (from a jar)
- 1/4 cup toasted almonds
- 1 garlic clove
- 2 tablespoons tomato paste
- 2 tablespoons olive oil
- 1 tablespoon red wine vinegar
- 1/2 teaspoon smoked paprika
- Salt and pepper, to taste

INSTRUCTIONS

1. Preheat your air fryer to 400°F (200°C).
2. Cut the cauliflower head into 1-inch thick slices, creating "cauliflower steaks." Reserve any florets that break off for another use.
3. In a small bowl, mix together olive oil, garlic powder, smoked paprika, salt, and pepper. Brush the mixture onto both sides of each cauliflower steak.
4. Place the cauliflower steaks in the air fryer basket and cook for 10 minutes. Flip the steaks halfway through the cooking time.
5. While the cauliflower is cooking, prepare the Romesco sauce. In a blender or food processor, combine roasted red bell peppers, toasted almonds, garlic clove, tomato paste, olive oil, red wine vinegar, smoked paprika, salt, and pepper. Blend until smooth.
6. Once the cauliflower steaks are done, transfer them to serving plates. Drizzle with the Romesco sauce and sprinkle with toasted almonds. Garnish with fresh parsley, if desired.
7. Serve the cauliflower steaks with your choice of side dishes or as a main course.

Nutrition Information (per serving): 250 Calories, 19g Fat, 17g Carbohydrates, 6g Protein, 7g Fiber.

Mushroom and Onion Pizzas with Vegan Cheese and Herbs

★ ☆ ☆ ☆ ☆

COOK TIME: 15 MINUTES

PREP TIME: 10 MINUTES

SERVINGS: 2

INGREDIENTS

- 2 large portobello mushroom caps
- 1 small red onion, thinly sliced
- 1/2 cup marinara sauce
- 1/2 cup vegan cheese, shredded
- 1 teaspoon dried oregano
- 1/2 teaspoon dried basil
- Salt and pepper, to taste
- Fresh basil leaves, for garnish (optional)

INSTRUCTIONS

1. Preheat your air fryer to 400°F (200°C).
2. Remove the stems from the portobello mushroom caps and gently scrape out the gills using a spoon. Place the mushroom caps in the air fryer basket.
3. Layer the thinly sliced red onion on top of the mushroom caps.
4. Spoon marinara sauce over the onion and mushroom caps, spreading it evenly.
5. Sprinkle vegan cheese over the sauce and top with dried oregano, dried basil, salt, and pepper.
6. Place the basket in the air fryer and cook for 12-15 minutes, or until the mushrooms are tender and the cheese is melted and bubbly.
7. Once cooked, remove the mushroom and onion pizzas from the air fryer and let them cool for a few minutes.
8. Garnish with fresh basil leaves, if desired, and serve hot.

Nutrition Information (per serving): 150 Calories, 7g Fat, 16g Carbohydrates, 7g Protein, 4g Fiber.

Sweet Potato and Kale Enchiladas with Red Sauce and Vegan Cheese

★★☆☆☆

COOK TIME: 25 MINUTES

PREP TIME: 20 MINUTES

SERVINGS: 4

INGREDIENTS

- 2 medium sweet potatoes, peeled and cubed
- 2 cups kale, stems removed and chopped
- 1 small onion, diced
- 2 cloves garlic, minced
- 1 tablespoon olive oil
- 1 teaspoon ground cumin
- 1/2 teaspoon chili powder
- Salt and pepper, to taste
- 8 small corn tortillas
- 1 cup red enchilada sauce
- 1 cup vegan cheese, shredded
- Fresh cilantro, for garnish (optional)

INSTRUCTIONS

1. Preheat your air fryer to 400°F (200°C).
2. In a large bowl, toss the sweet potato cubes with olive oil, ground cumin, chili powder, salt, and pepper until well coated.
3. Place the seasoned sweet potatoes in the air fryer basket and cook for 15-20 minutes, or until they are tender and lightly browned.
4. While the sweet potatoes are cooking, heat a pan over medium heat and sauté the onion and garlic until they become translucent.
5. Add the chopped kale to the pan and cook until wilted, about 3-4 minutes. Season with salt and pepper to taste. Once the sweet potatoes are cooked, remove them from the air fryer and transfer them to a bowl. Mash them lightly with a fork.
6. Warm the corn tortillas in a microwave or on a stovetop until they are pliable.
7. Spread a spoonful of mashed sweet potatoes onto each tortilla, followed by a spoonful of the kale and onion mixture. Roll up the tortillas and place them seam-side down in the air fryer basket.
8. Pour the red enchilada sauce over the enchiladas and sprinkle vegan cheese on top.
9. Place the basket back into the air fryer and cook for another 5 minutes, or until the enchiladas are heated through and the cheese is melted.

Nutrition Information (per serving): 290 Calories, 10g Fat, 45g Carbohydrates, 8g Protein, 7g Fiber.

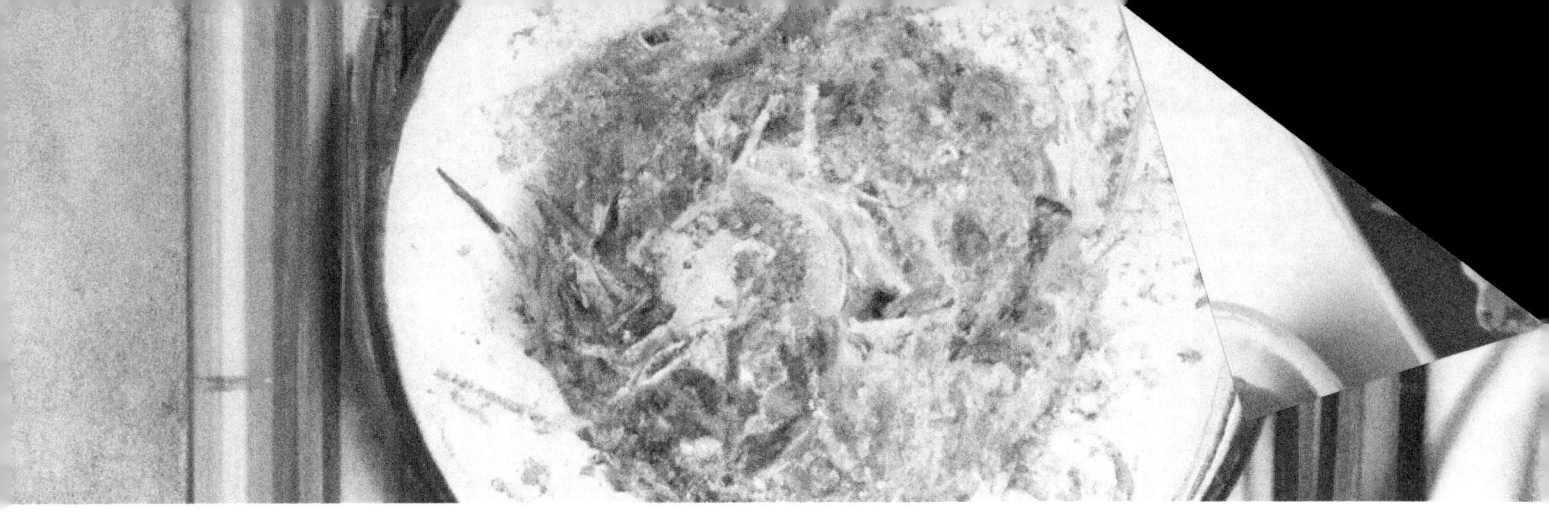

Pad Thai with Rice Noodles and Peanut Sauce

★★★★☆

COOK TIME: 15 MINUTES

PREP TIME: 15 MINUTES

SERVINGS: 2

INGREDIENTS

- 4 ounces rice noodles
- 1 tablespoon vegetable oil
- 1/2 cup tofu, diced
- 1/4 cup shallots, thinly sliced
- 2 cloves garlic, minced
- 1/2 cup carrots, julienned
- 1/2 cup bell peppers, thinly sliced
- 1/2 cup bean sprouts
- 2 tablespoons soy sauce
- 1 tablespoon lime juice
- 1 tablespoon peanut butter
- 1 tablespoon maple syrup
- 1/4 teaspoon red pepper flakes (optional)
- 2 tablespoons chopped peanuts, for garnish
- Fresh cilantro, for garnish (optional)
- Lime wedges, for serving

INSTRUCTIONS

1. Cook the rice noodles according to package instructions. Drain and set aside.
2. Preheat the air fryer to 400°F (200°C).
3. In a small bowl, whisk together soy sauce, lime juice, peanut butter, maple syrup, and red pepper flakes (if using) to make the peanut sauce. Set aside.
4. Heat the vegetable oil in a pan over medium heat. Add tofu and cook until it becomes crispy and golden brown on all sides. Remove from the pan and set aside.
5. In the same pan, add shallots, garlic, carrots, and bell peppers. Sauté for 2-3 minutes until the vegetables are slightly softened.
6. Transfer the sautéed vegetables to the air fryer basket and cook for 5-6 minutes, shaking the basket occasionally, until the vegetables are tender and lightly charred.
7. Add the cooked rice noodles, bean sprouts, and peanut sauce to the air fryer basket. Toss everything together until well coated.
8. Cook for an additional 2-3 minutes, until the noodles are heated through.
9. Divide the Pad Thai among plates or bowls. Garnish with chopped peanuts and fresh cilantro (if desired). Serve with lime wedges on the side.

Nutrition Information (per serving): 530 Calories, 18g Fat, 77g Carbohydrates, 16g Protein, 5g Fiber.

Zucchini and Tomato Gratin with Cheese and Herbs

★★☆☆☆

COOK TIME: 25 MINUTES

PREP TIME: 15 MINUTES

SERVINGS: 4

INGREDIENTS

- 2 medium zucchini, sliced
- 2 medium tomatoes, sliced
- 1/2 cup vegan cheese, grated
- 1/4 cup breadcrumbs
- 2 tablespoons fresh basil, chopped
- 1 tablespoon fresh thyme leaves
- 2 tablespoons olive oil
- Salt and pepper to taste

INSTRUCTIONS

1. Preheat the air fryer to 375°F (190°C).
2. In a mixing bowl, combine the zucchini slices, tomato slices, olive oil, fresh basil, and fresh thyme leaves. Season with salt and pepper to taste. Toss everything together to coat the vegetables evenly.
3. Place the zucchini and tomato mixture in the air fryer basket. Spread it out in an even layer.
4. Air fry for 10 minutes. After 10 minutes, sprinkle the vegan cheese and breadcrumbs over the top of the vegetables.
5. Continue to air fry for another 10-15 minutes, or until the zucchini is tender and the cheese is melted and golden brown.
6. Once cooked, remove the gratin from the air fryer and let it cool for a few minutes before serving.
7. Serve warm as a side dish or a light main course.

Nutrition Information (per serving): 150 Calories, 10g Fat, 12g Carbohydrates, 4g Protein, 3g Fiber.

BBQ Tofu and Vegetable Skewers with Barbecue Sauce

★ ★ ★ ☆ ☆

COOK TIME: 20 MINUTES

PREP TIME: 15 MINUTES

SERVINGS: 4

INGREDIENTS

- 1 block of tofu, pressed and cut into cubes
- 1 red bell pepper, cut into chunks
- 1 yellow bell pepper, cut into chunks
- 1 zucchini, sliced
- 1 red onion, cut into chunks
- 1/2 cup barbecue sauce
- 2 tablespoons olive oil
- Salt and pepper to taste
- Skewers, soaked in water if using wooden skewers

INSTRUCTIONS

1. Preheat the air fryer to 400°F (200°C).
2. In a bowl, combine the tofu cubes, bell peppers, zucchini, red onion, olive oil, barbecue sauce, salt, and pepper. Toss everything together to coat the tofu and vegetables with the sauce.
3. Thread the tofu and vegetables onto the skewers, alternating between them.
4. Place the skewers in the air fryer basket in a single layer, making sure they are not overcrowded.
5. Air fry for 10 minutes, then flip the skewers and air fry for another 10 minutes, or until the tofu is crispy and the vegetables are tender.
6. Remove the skewers from the air fryer and let them cool for a few minutes before serving.
7. Serve the BBQ tofu and vegetable skewers with extra barbecue sauce on the side, if desired.

Nutrition Information (per serving): 220 Calories, 8g Fat, 28g Carbohydrates, 11g Protein, 5g Fiber.

Stuffed Bell Peppers with Quinoa, Black Beans and Cheese

★★☆☆☆

COOK TIME: 25 MINUTES

PREP TIME: 15 MINUTES

SERVINGS: 4

INGREDIENTS

- 4 bell peppers (any color), tops removed and seeds removed
- 1 cup cooked quinoa
- 1 cup cooked black beans
- 1 cup shredded cheese (such as cheddar or mozzarella)
- 1/2 cup diced tomatoes
- 1/4 cup diced onion
- 2 cloves garlic, minced
- 1 tablespoon olive oil
- 1 teaspoon cumin
- 1/2 teaspoon paprika
- Salt and pepper to taste

INSTRUCTIONS

1. Preheat the air fryer to 375°F (190°C).
2. In a large bowl, combine the cooked quinoa, black beans, diced tomatoes, onion, garlic, olive oil, cumin, paprika, salt, and pepper. Mix well.
3. Stuff each bell pepper with the quinoa and black bean mixture, pressing it down gently. Top each pepper with shredded cheese.
4. Place the stuffed bell peppers in the air fryer basket.
5. Air fry for 20-25 minutes, or until the peppers are tender and the cheese is melted and slightly golden.
6. Remove the stuffed bell peppers from the air fryer and let them cool for a few minutes before serving.

Nutrition Information (per serving): 300 Calories, 10g Fat, 39g Carbohydrates, 16g Protein, 10g Fiber.

Lentil and Vegetable Shepherd's Pie with Mashed Potatoes

★★☆☆☆

COOK TIME: 30 MINUTES

PREP TIME: 20 MINUTES

SERVINGS: 4

INGREDIENTS

For the lentil and vegetable filling:
- 1 cup lentils, cooked
- 1 tablespoon olive oil
- 1 onion, chopped
- 2 cloves garlic, minced
- 2 carrots, diced
- 1 celery stalk, diced
- 1 bell pepper, diced
- 1 zucchini, diced
- 1 cup frozen peas
- 1 teaspoon dried thyme
- 1 teaspoon dried rosemary
- 1 tablespoon tomato paste
- 1 cup vegetable broth
- Salt and pepper to taste

For the mashed potatoes:
- 4 large potatoes, peeled and chopped
- 1/4 cup non-dairy milk (such as almond or soy milk)
- 2 tablespoons vegan butter
- Salt and pepper to taste

INSTRUCTIONS

1. Preheat the air fryer to 400°F (200°C).
2. Heat olive oil in a large skillet over medium heat. Add the onion and garlic and cook until softened and fragrant.
3. Add the carrots, celery, bell pepper, and zucchini to the skillet. Cook for 5-7 minutes, until the vegetables are slightly tender.
4. Stir in the cooked lentils, frozen peas, dried thyme, dried rosemary, tomato paste, and vegetable broth. Cook for another 5 minutes, until the mixture is heated through and the flavors are well combined. Season with salt and pepper to taste.
5. Meanwhile, cook the chopped potatoes in a pot of boiling water until tender. Drain the potatoes and return them to the pot.
6. Mash the potatoes with a potato masher or fork. Add non-dairy milk, vegan butter, salt, and pepper. Continue mashing until the potatoes are smooth and creamy.
7. Transfer the lentil and vegetable filling to a baking dish. Spread the mashed potatoes evenly over the top.
8. Place the baking dish in the air fryer and cook for 15 minutes, or until the mashed potatoes are golden and crispy.

Nutrition Information (per serving): 350 Calories, 8g Fat, 60g Carbohydrates, 14g Protein, 14g Fiber.

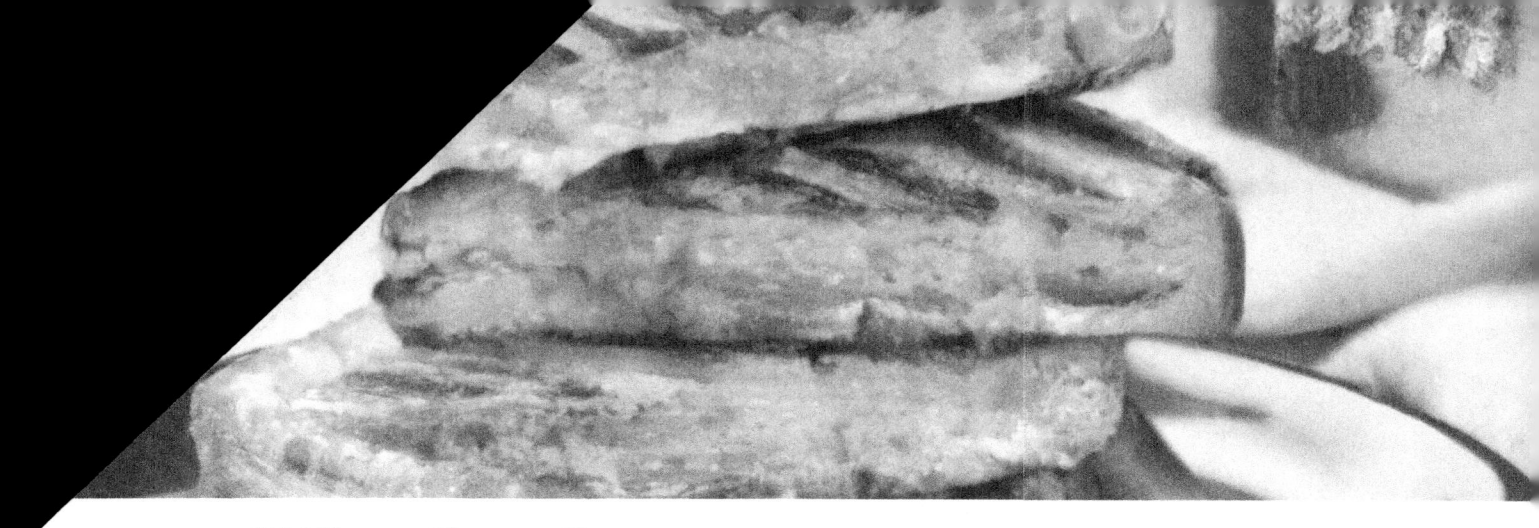

Grilled Cheese Sandwich

★ ☆ ☆ ☆ ☆

COOK TIME: 8 MINUTES

PREP TIME: 5 MINUTES

SERVINGS: 1

INGREDIENTS

- 2 slices of bread (vegan)
- 1/4 cup vegan cheese, shredded
- 1 tbsp vegan butter
- **Optional:** vegan mayo, mustard, tomato, or any other toppings you like

INSTRUCTIONS

1. Preheat your air fryer to 375°F (190°C).
2. Butter one side of each slice of bread and place one slice, buttered side down, on a cutting board or plate.
3. Sprinkle the shredded cheese over the slice of bread and place the other slice on top, buttered side up.
4. Place the sandwich in the air fryer basket and cook for 4 minutes.
5. Flip the sandwich over and cook for an additional 3-4 minutes, or until the bread is golden brown and the cheese is melted.
6. Remove the sandwich from the air fryer and let it cool for a minute or two before slicing and serving.
7. If desired, add any additional toppings like vegan mayo, mustard, or sliced tomato.

Nutrition Information (per serving): 300 Calories, 12g Fat, 35g Carbohydrates, 10g Protein, 4g Fiber.

Seitan and Vegetable Skewers with Lemon and Herbs

★★☆☆☆

COOK TIME: 15 MINUTES

PREP TIME: 20 MINUTES

SERVINGS: 4

INGREDIENTS

- 1/2 pound seitan, cut into 1-inch cubes
- 2 bell peppers, seeded and cut into 1-inch pieces
- 1 zucchini, sliced into 1/4-inch rounds
- 1 red onion, cut into 1-inch pieces
- 1/4 cup olive oil
- 2 tablespoons fresh lemon juice
- 2 garlic cloves, minced
- 1 tablespoon dried oregano
- Salt and pepper to taste
- Skewers

INSTRUCTIONS

1. Preheat the air fryer to 375°F.
2. Thread the seitan, bell peppers, zucchini, and red onion onto the skewers.
3. In a small bowl, whisk together the olive oil, lemon juice, garlic, oregano, salt, and pepper.
4. Brush the skewers with the olive oil mixture.
5. Place the skewers in the air fryer basket and cook for 15 minutes, flipping halfway through.
6. Serve hot with additional lemon wedges, if desired.

Nutrition Information (per serving): 275 Calories, 16g Fat, 14g Carbohydrates, 19g Protein, 4g Fiber.

CHAPTER 3. MAIN DISHES / 79

Butternut Squash and Sage Lasagna with Vegan Cheese

★★★★☆

COOK TIME: 40 MINUTES

PREP TIME: 30 MINUTES

SERVINGS: 4

INGREDIENTS

- 6 whole wheat lasagna noodles
- 2 cups butternut squash, peeled and cubed
- 1 tbsp olive oil
- 1 onion, chopped
- 2 cloves garlic, minced
- 2 cups spinach, chopped
- 2 tbsp fresh sage, chopped
- 1 tsp dried oregano
- 1/4 tsp salt
- 1/4 tsp black pepper
- 1 1/2 cups marinara sauce
- 1/2 cup vegan ricotta cheese
- 1/2 cup vegan mozzarella cheese, shredded

INSTRUCTIONS

1. Preheat the air fryer to 350°F (180°C).
2. Cook the lasagna noodles according to the package instructions until al dente. Drain and rinse with cold water.
3. In a bowl, toss the butternut squash with olive oil and season with salt and black pepper. Place the squash in the air fryer basket and cook for 15-20 minutes, until tender and lightly browned.
4. In a pan, sauté the onion and garlic until soft and fragrant. Add the spinach, sage, oregano, salt, and black pepper, and cook for 2-3 minutes until the spinach is wilted.
5. In a small bowl, mix the vegan ricotta cheese with 1/2 cup of the marinara sauce.
6. In a baking dish, spread 1/4 cup of the marinara sauce on the bottom. Place 2 cooked lasagna noodles on top of the sauce. Add 1/3 of the butternut squash, 1/3 of the spinach mixture, and 1/3 of the ricotta mixture on top of the noodles. Repeat the layers, ending with the remaining noodles on top.
7. Pour the remaining marinara sauce over the lasagna noodles and top with shredded vegan mozzarella cheese.
8. Place the baking dish in the air fryer basket and cook at 350°F (180°C) for 20-25 minutes, until the cheese is melted and bubbly.
9. Remove the lasagna from the air fryer and let it cool for 5 minutes before slicing and serving.

Nutrition Information (per serving): 356 Calories, 16.3g Fat, 38.1g Carbohydrates, 16.1g Protein, 8.6g Fiber

Chickpea and Vegetable Burgers with Buns and Fixings

★★☆☆☆

COOK TIME: 15 MINUTES

PREP TIME: 20 MINUTES

SERVINGS: 4

INGREDIENTS

- 1 can of chickpeas, drained and rinsed
- 1/2 red onion, chopped
- 1/2 red bell pepper, chopped
- 1/2 cup of breadcrumbs
- 1 tbsp of ground flaxseed mixed with 3 tbsp of water
- 1 tsp of smoked paprika
- 1 tsp of cumin
- 1/4 tsp of salt
- 4 whole grain burger buns
- Lettuce, tomato, avocado, and other fixings as desired

INSTRUCTIONS

1. Preheat the air fryer to 375°F.
2. In a food processor, pulse together the chickpeas, red onion, red bell pepper, breadcrumbs, ground flaxseed mixture, smoked paprika, cumin, and salt until combined.
3. Divide the mixture into 4 equal portions and form each into a patty.
4. Place the patties in the air fryer and cook for 7-8 minutes on each side until golden brown and crispy.
5. Toast the burger buns and assemble the burgers with lettuce, tomato, avocado, and other fixings as desired.

Nutrition Information (per serving): 360 Calories, 7g Fat, 61g Carbohydrates, 16g Protein, 12g Fiber

Stuffed Portobello Mushrooms with Quinoa, Spinach and Vegan Cheese

★★★☆☆

COOK TIME: 15 MINUTES

PREP TIME: 20 MINUTES

SERVINGS: 4

INGREDIENTS

- 4 large portobello mushrooms
- 1 cup cooked quinoa
- 1 cup fresh spinach, chopped
- 1/2 cup vegan cheese, shredded
- 2 cloves garlic, minced
- 1/2 teaspoon salt
- 1/4 teaspoon black pepper
- 1 tablespoon olive oil

INSTRUCTIONS

1. Preheat the air fryer to 375°F (190°C).
2. Clean the mushrooms and remove the stems.
3. In a large mixing bowl, combine cooked quinoa, chopped spinach, minced garlic, salt and black pepper. Mix well.
4. Stuff each mushroom with the quinoa and spinach mixture.
5. Sprinkle vegan cheese over the top of each stuffed mushroom.
6. Brush the mushroom caps with olive oil.
7. Place the stuffed mushrooms in the air fryer basket.
8. Cook for 15 minutes, until the mushrooms are tender and the cheese is melted.
9. Serve hot and enjoy!

Nutrition Information (per serving): 170 Calories, 9.4g Fat, 15.6g Carbohydrates, 8g Protein, 3.8g Fiber

Chapter 4

Sides and Salads

Roasted Carrots with Honey and Thyme

★ ★ ☆ ☆ ☆

COOK TIME: 15 MINUTES

PREP TIME: 5 MINUTES

SERVINGS: 4

INGREDIENTS

- 1 lb. carrots, peeled and sliced into long sticks
- 1 tbsp. olive oil
- 1 tbsp. honey (or maple syrup for a vegan alternative)
- 1 tsp. fresh thyme leaves
- Salt and pepper, to taste

INSTRUCTIONS

1. Preheat your air fryer to 400°F.
2. In a large bowl, toss the sliced carrots with olive oil, honey, thyme, salt, and pepper until evenly coated.
3. Place the carrots in the air fryer basket in a single layer.
4. Cook for 10-15 minutes, or until the carrots are tender and golden brown, shaking the basket every 5 minutes to ensure even cooking.
5. Serve hot and enjoy!

Nutrition Information (per serving): 90 Calories, 3g Fat, 16g Carbohydrates, 1g Protein, 3g Fiber

Grilled Corn on the Cob with Chili Powder and Lime

★ ☆ ☆ ☆ ☆

COOK TIME: 10-12 MINUTES

PREP TIME: 5 MINUTES

SERVINGS: 4

INGREDIENTS

- 4 ears of corn, husks and silks removed
- 1 tbsp olive oil
- 1 tsp chili powder
- 1/2 tsp garlic powder
- Salt and pepper to taste
- Juice of 1 lime

INSTRUCTIONS

1. Preheat the air fryer to 375°F (190°C).
2. Brush the corn with olive oil.
3. In a small bowl, mix together the chili powder, garlic powder, salt, and pepper.
4. Sprinkle the spice mix over the corn, making sure it is evenly coated.
5. Place the corn in the air fryer basket and cook for 10-12 minutes, turning halfway through, until the corn is tender and lightly browned.
6. Squeeze the lime juice over the corn and serve.

Nutrition Information (per serving): 107 Calories, 4g Fat, 19g Carbohydrates, 3g Protein, 3g Fiber

Baked Potato Wedges with Rosemary and Sea Salt

★★☆☆☆

COOK TIME: 25 MINUTES

PREP TIME: 10 MINUTES

SERVINGS: 4

INGREDIENTS

- 4 large potatoes, cut into wedges
- 2 tbsp olive oil
- 2 tbsp fresh rosemary, chopped
- 1 tsp sea salt

INSTRUCTIONS

1. Preheat the air fryer to 400°F (200°C).
2. In a bowl, mix together the potato wedges, olive oil, rosemary, and salt until the wedges are coated evenly.
3. Place the wedges in a single layer in the air fryer basket.
4. Cook for 20-25 minutes, shaking the basket every 5-10 minutes, until the wedges are crispy and golden brown.
5. Serve hot.

Nutrition Information (per serving): 202 Calories, 7g Fat, 32g Carbohydrates, 4g Protein, 4g Fiber

Roasted Brussels Sprouts with Balsamic Vinegar and Maple Syrup

★★✩✩✩

COOK TIME: 10 MINUTES

PREP TIME: 5 MINUTES

SERVINGS: 4

INGREDIENTS

- 1 pound Brussels sprouts, trimmed and halved
- 1 tablespoon olive oil
- Salt and pepper to taste
- 2 tablespoons balsamic vinegar
- 1 tablespoon maple syrup

INSTRUCTIONS

1. Preheat the air fryer to 375°F.
2. In a large mixing bowl, toss the Brussels sprouts with olive oil, salt, and pepper until well coated.
3. Place the Brussels sprouts in the air fryer basket and cook for 8 minutes.
4. In a small bowl, whisk together balsamic vinegar and maple syrup.
5. After 8 minutes, drizzle the balsamic mixture over the Brussels sprouts and give the basket a gentle shake to coat the sprouts.
6. Return the basket to the air fryer and cook for an additional 2-3 minutes or until the Brussels sprouts are crispy and tender.
7. Serve hot and enjoy!

Nutrition Information (per serving): 78 Calories, 3.5g Fat, 12g Carbohydrates, 3g Protein, 4g Fiber

Sweet Potato Fries with Garlic Aioli

★★☆☆☆

COOK TIME: 15-20 MINUTES

PREP TIME: 10 MINUTES

SERVINGS: 4

INGREDIENTS

- 2 large sweet potatoes, cut into fries
- 1 tbsp cornstarch
- 1 tbsp olive oil
- 1/2 tsp garlic powder
- 1/2 tsp paprika
- Salt and pepper, to taste

For the garlic aioli:

- 1/2 cup vegan mayonnaise
- 2 garlic cloves, minced
- 1 tbsp lemon juice
- Salt and pepper, to taste

INSTRUCTIONS

1. Preheat the air fryer to 400°F (200°C).
2. In a bowl, toss the sweet potato fries with cornstarch, olive oil, garlic powder, paprika, salt, and pepper until coated evenly.
3. Place the sweet potato fries in the air fryer basket and cook for 15-20 minutes or until crispy, shaking the basket halfway through.
4. While the fries are cooking, prepare the garlic aioli. In a small bowl, whisk together the vegan mayonnaise, minced garlic, lemon juice, salt, and pepper.
5. Serve the sweet potato fries hot with the garlic aioli on the side.

Nutrition Information (per serving): Calories: 213, Fat: 12g, Carbohydrates: 26g, Protein: 2g, Fiber: 4g

Grilled Asparagus with Lemon and Olive Oil

★★☆☆☆

COOK TIME: 8-10 MINUTES

PREP TIME: 10 MINUTES

SERVINGS: 4

INGREDIENTS

- 1 pound asparagus, trimmed
- 1 tablespoon olive oil
- 1/2 teaspoon salt
- 1/4 teaspoon black pepper
- 1 lemon, zested and juiced

INSTRUCTIONS

1. Preheat air fryer to 400°F.
2. In a large bowl, toss asparagus with olive oil, salt, and black pepper.
3. Place asparagus in the air fryer basket in a single layer.
4. Cook for 8-10 minutes, shaking the basket occasionally, until asparagus is tender and lightly charred.
5. Remove from air fryer and transfer to a serving plate.
6. Drizzle lemon juice over the asparagus and sprinkle with lemon zest.
7. Serve immediately.

Nutrition Information (per serving): Calories: 50, Fat: 3.5g, Carbohydrates: 4g, Protein: 2g, Fiber: 2g

Cauliflower Rice with Turmeric and Cumin

★ ★ ★ ☆ ☆

COOK TIME: 15 MINUTES

PREP TIME: 10 MINUTES

SERVINGS: 4

INGREDIENTS

- 1 head of cauliflower
- 1 tablespoon olive oil
- 1 teaspoon ground turmeric
- 1 teaspoon ground cumin
- Salt and pepper to taste
- Fresh cilantro for garnish

INSTRUCTIONS

1. Cut the cauliflower into small florets and pulse in a food processor until it resembles rice.
2. In a mixing bowl, toss the cauliflower rice with olive oil, turmeric, cumin, salt, and pepper.
3. Preheat the air fryer to 380°F (190°C).
4. Add the seasoned cauliflower rice to the air fryer basket and cook for 10-15 minutes, shaking the basket every 5 minutes to ensure even cooking.
5. Once cooked, garnish with fresh cilantro and serve hot.

Nutrition Information (per serving): Calories: 50, Fat: 3g, Carbohydrates: 6g, Protein: 2g, Fiber: 3g

Roasted Butternut Squash with Cinnamon and Maple Syrup

★ ★ ★ ☆ ☆

COOK TIME: 15 MINUTES

PREP TIME: 10 MINUTES

SERVINGS: 4

INGREDIENTS

- 1 small butternut squash, peeled and cubed
- 1 tablespoon olive oil
- 1 teaspoon cinnamon
- 1 tablespoon maple syrup
- Salt and pepper to taste

INSTRUCTIONS

1. Preheat your air fryer to 400°F (200°C).
2. In a mixing bowl, toss the cubed butternut squash with olive oil, cinnamon, and salt and pepper.
3. Place the seasoned butternut squash in the air fryer basket in a single layer.
4. Air fry for 10 minutes.
5. Remove the basket from the air fryer and drizzle the maple syrup over the butternut squash.
6. Toss to coat evenly.
7. Return the basket to the air fryer and air fry for an additional 5 minutes.
8. Serve hot.

Nutrition Information (per serving): Calories: 85 kcal, Fat: 3.5g, Carbohydrates: 15g, Protein: 1g, Fiber: 2.5g

Baked Sweet Potato with Cinnamon and Coconut Oil

★★☆☆☆

COOK TIME: 35 MINUTES

PREP TIME: 5 MINUTES

SERVINGS: 2

INGREDIENTS

- 2 medium sweet potatoes, washed and dried
- 1 tablespoon melted coconut oil
- 1 teaspoon ground cinnamon
- Salt, to taste

INSTRUCTIONS

1. Preheat the air fryer to 375°F (190°C).
2. Pierce each sweet potato several times with a fork.
3. Rub the sweet potatoes with coconut oil and sprinkle with cinnamon and salt.
4. Place the sweet potatoes in the air fryer basket and cook for 30-35 minutes, or until they are tender and the skin is crispy.
5. Serve immediately, topped with additional coconut oil or vegan butter and sprinkle with cinnamon, if desired.

Nutrition Information (per serving): Calories: 180, Fat: 6g, Carbohydrates: 32g, Protein: 2g, Fiber: 5g

Grilled Zucchini with Balsamic Vinegar and Basil

★ ★ ☆ ☆ ☆

COOK TIME: 10 MINUTES

PREP TIME: 10 MINUTES

SERVINGS: 4

INGREDIENTS

- 2 medium zucchinis, sliced into 1/4-inch rounds
- 2 tbsp olive oil
- Salt and pepper to taste
- 2 tbsp balsamic vinegar
- 1 tbsp fresh chopped basil

INSTRUCTIONS

1. Preheat the air fryer to 400°F (200°C).
2. In a bowl, toss zucchini rounds with olive oil, salt, and pepper.
3. Place the zucchini rounds in the air fryer basket in a single layer.
4. Air fry for 5 minutes. Flip the zucchini rounds and air fry for an additional 5 minutes.
5. Remove the zucchini rounds from the air fryer basket and transfer to a serving dish.
6. Drizzle balsamic vinegar over the zucchini rounds and sprinkle with fresh basil.
7. Serve hot.

Nutrition Information (per serving): Calories: 85, Fat: 7g, Carbohydrates: 6g, Protein: 1g, Fiber: 2g

Fried Rice with Vegetables and Soy Sauce

★★ ★ ★ ★ **COOK TIME:** 15 MINUTES   **PREP TIME:** 10 MINUTES   **SERVINGS:** 4

INGREDIENTS

- 2 cups cooked brown rice
- 1 tbsp vegetable oil
- 1/2 cup diced onion
- 1/2 cup diced carrot
- 1/2 cup diced celery
- 1 cup diced mixed vegetables (such as peas, corn, and bell pepper)
- 2 cloves garlic, minced
- 2 tbsp soy sauce
- 1/4 tsp black pepper
- 1/4 tsp red pepper flakes (optional)

INSTRUCTIONS

1. Preheat your air fryer to 370°F.
2. Heat the vegetable oil in a large skillet over medium heat. Add the onion, carrot, and celery and cook until softened, about 5 minutes.
3. Add the mixed vegetables and garlic to the skillet and cook for another 5 minutes, until the vegetables are tender.
4. Add the cooked rice to the skillet and stir to combine with the vegetables.
5. Drizzle the soy sauce over the rice and stir to evenly distribute.
6. Transfer the rice and vegetable mixture to the air fryer basket and sprinkle with black pepper and red pepper flakes (if using).
7. Air fry for 10 minutes, stirring halfway through cooking time.
8. Serve hot and enjoy!

Nutrition Information (per serving): Calories: 194, Fat: 5g, Carbohydrates: 34g, Protein: 5g, Fiber: 4g

Roasted Bell Peppers with Oregano and Garlic

★★☆☆☆

COOK TIME: 10 MINUTES

PREP TIME: 10 MINUTES

SERVINGS: 4

INGREDIENTS

- 2 bell peppers, sliced into strips
- 1 tablespoon olive oil
- 1 teaspoon dried oregano
- 2 cloves garlic, minced
- Salt and black pepper to taste

INSTRUCTIONS

1. Preheat the air fryer to 400°F (200°C).
2. In a mixing bowl, toss the bell pepper strips with olive oil, oregano, garlic, salt, and black pepper.
3. Arrange the seasoned bell pepper strips in a single layer in the air fryer basket.
4. Cook the bell pepper strips in the air fryer for 8-10 minutes or until they are crispy and golden brown, shaking the basket halfway through.
5. Serve hot as a side dish or topping for salads, sandwiches, or wraps.

Nutrition Information (per serving): Calories: 45, Fat: 3g, Carbohydrates: 5g, Protein: 1g, Fiber: 2g

Quinoa Salad with Avocado, Cilantro, and Lime

★★ ☆ ☆ ☆

COOK TIME: 15 MINUTES

PREP TIME: 10 MINUTES

SERVINGS: 4

INGREDIENTS

- 1 cup quinoa, rinsed and drained
- 2 cups water
- 1 avocado, diced
- 1/2 red onion, diced
- 1/2 cup cilantro, chopped
- 1 lime, juiced
- 1 tablespoon olive oil
- Salt and pepper to taste

INSTRUCTIONS

1. In a medium saucepan, bring quinoa and water to a boil over medium-high heat. Reduce heat to low, cover, and simmer for 15 minutes, or until quinoa is tender and water is absorbed.
2. Preheat the air fryer to 400°F (200°C).
3. In a large bowl, combine cooked quinoa, avocado, red onion, cilantro, lime juice, olive oil, salt, and pepper.
4. Toss the quinoa mixture to combine all ingredients.
5. Place the quinoa mixture in the air fryer basket and cook for 5-7 minutes, or until the edges of the avocado and quinoa begin to brown.
6. Serve and enjoy!

Nutrition Information (per serving): Calories 296; Fat 15g; Carbohydrates 33g; Protein 8g

Grilled Eggplant with Balsamic Vinegar and Mint

★☆☆☆☆

COOK TIME: 15 MINUTES

PREP TIME: 10 MINUTES

SERVINGS: 4

INGREDIENTS

- 1 large eggplant, sliced into rounds
- 2 tbsp olive oil
- Salt and pepper, to taste
- 1/4 cup balsamic vinegar
- 2 tbsp fresh mint, chopped

INSTRUCTIONS

1. Preheat the air fryer to 375°F.
2. Brush eggplant slices with olive oil and sprinkle with salt and pepper.
3. Place eggplant slices in the air fryer basket in a single layer.
4. Air fry for 10 minutes, flipping halfway through.
5. Drizzle balsamic vinegar over the eggplant slices and air fry for an additional 5 minutes.
6. Remove the eggplant from the air fryer and sprinkle with fresh mint.
7. Serve hot.

Nutrition Information (per serving): Calories: 97; Fat: 7.6g; Carbs: 7.4g; Protein: 1.4g; Fiber: 3.5g; Sugar: 5.2g; Sodium: 5.2mg

Coleslaw with Vegan Mayo and Vinegar

★★☆☆☆

COOK TIME: 10 MINUTES

PREP TIME: 15 MINUTES

SERVINGS: 4

INGREDIENTS

- 4 cups shredded cabbage
- 1/2 cup grated carrot
- 1/4 cup diced onion
- 1/2 cup vegan mayonnaise
- 2 tablespoons white vinegar
- 1 tablespoon dijon mustard
- 1 tablespoon agave nectar
- Salt and pepper to taste

INSTRUCTIONS

1. In a bowl, mix together the cabbage, carrot, and onion.
2. In a separate bowl, whisk together the vegan mayonnaise, white vinegar, dijon mustard, and agave nectar.
3. Pour the dressing over the cabbage mixture and toss to combine.
4. Season with salt and pepper to taste.
5. Place the coleslaw mixture in the air fryer basket and cook at 375°F for 10 minutes, tossing halfway through.
6. Serve and enjoy!

Nutrition Information (per serving): Calories 146; Fat 13g; Saturated Fat 1g; Carbohydrates 8g; Fiber 3g; Sugar 5g; Protein 1g

Pasta Salad with Vegetables and Vinaigrette

★★★☆☆

COOK TIME: 15 MINUTES

PREP TIME: 10 MINUTES

SERVINGS: 4

INGREDIENTS

- 8 oz pasta, cooked according to package instructions
- 1 red bell pepper, chopped
- 1 yellow bell pepper, chopped
- 1 small red onion, chopped
- 1 small zucchini, chopped
- 1 small yellow squash, chopped
- 1/4 cup chopped fresh parsley
- 1/4 cup chopped fresh basil
- Salt and pepper to taste
- 1/4 cup olive oil
- 2 tablespoons red wine vinegar
- 1 tablespoon Dijon mustard
- 1 garlic clove, minced

INSTRUCTIONS

1. Preheat the air fryer to 350°F.
2. In a bowl, whisk together the olive oil, red wine vinegar, Dijon mustard, and garlic.
3. In another bowl, combine the cooked pasta, chopped vegetables, parsley, and basil.
4. Pour the dressing over the pasta and vegetables, and toss to coat evenly.
5. Place the pasta mixture in the air fryer basket and cook for 5-7 minutes or until vegetables are slightly tender.
6. Season with salt and pepper to taste and serve.

Nutrition Information (per serving): 396 calories, 21g fat, 45g carbohydrates, 9g protein, 4g fiber

Grilled Peaches with Cinnamon and Honey

★ ☆ ☆ ☆ ☆

COOK TIME:
10 MINUTES

PREP TIME:
10 MINUTES

SERVINGS:
4

INGREDIENTS

- 4 ripe peaches, halved and pitted
- 1 tablespoon honey
- 1/2 teaspoon cinnamon
- Cooking spray

INSTRUCTIONS

1. Preheat the air fryer to 375°F.
2. Spray the air fryer basket with cooking spray.
3. Place the peach halves in the basket, cut side up.
4. Drizzle the honey over the peaches.
5. Sprinkle the cinnamon over the peaches.
6. Air fry for 8 minutes or until the peaches are tender and caramelized.
7. Serve warm.

Nutrition Information (per serving): Calories: 87; Fat: 0.4g; Carbohydrates: 22.1g; Fiber: 2.6g; Protein: 1.6g

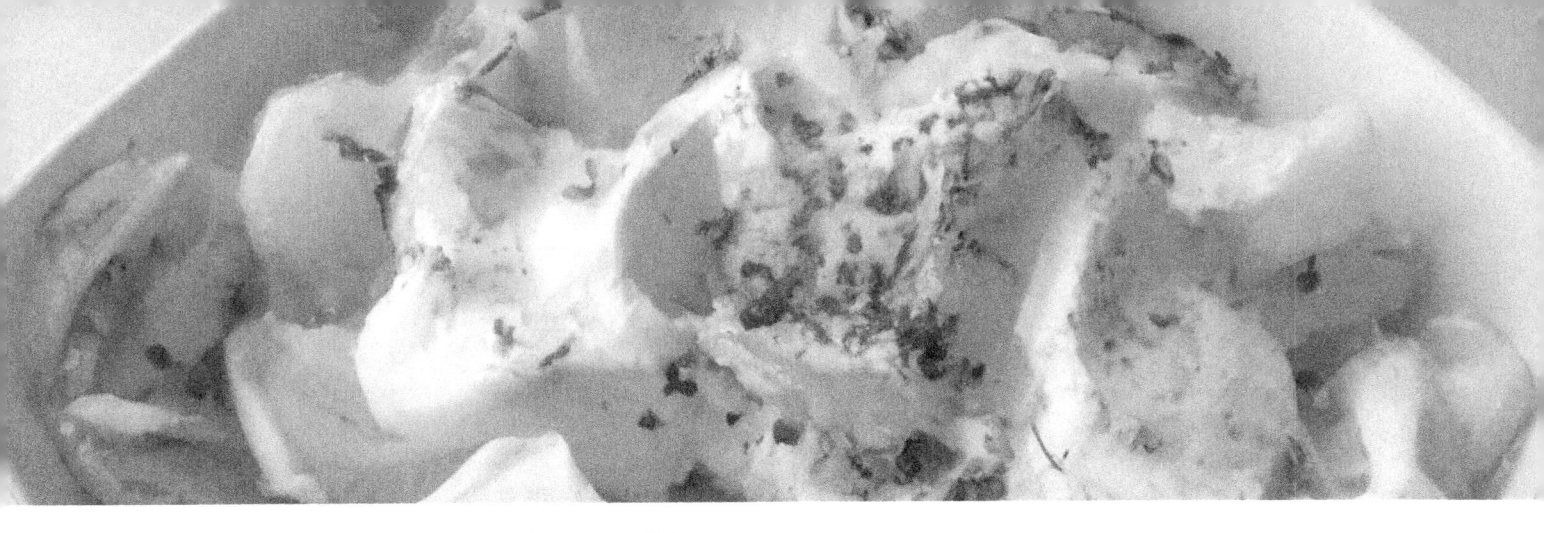

Potato Salad with Vegan Mayo and Herbs

★ ★ ☆ ☆ ☆

COOK TIME: 20 MINUTES

PREP TIME: 10 MINUTES

SERVINGS: 4

INGREDIENTS

- 1 1/2 pounds baby potatoes, halved
- 1/4 cup vegan mayonnaise
- 2 tablespoons Dijon mustard
- 2 tablespoons apple cider vinegar
- 2 tablespoons chopped fresh parsley
- 2 tablespoons chopped fresh chives
- Salt and pepper to taste

INSTRUCTIONS

1. Preheat the air fryer to 400°F (200°C).
2. Place the halved potatoes in the air fryer basket and cook for 20 minutes, shaking the basket every 5 minutes, until the potatoes are crispy and tender.
3. In a small bowl, whisk together the vegan mayonnaise, Dijon mustard, apple cider vinegar, parsley, and chives until well combined.
4. Once the potatoes are done, transfer them to a large mixing bowl and add the dressing. Toss until the potatoes are well coated.
5. Season with salt and pepper to taste.
6. Chill in the refrigerator for at least 30 minutes before serving.

Nutrition Information (per serving): Calories: 186 kcal, Fat: 4.4 g, Carbohydrates: 33.6 g, Protein: 3.6 g, Fiber: 3.9 g

Roasted Radishes with Butter and Sea Salt

★ ☆ ☆ ☆ ☆

COOK TIME: 10 MINUTES

PREP TIME: 5 MINUTES

SERVINGS: 2

INGREDIENTS

- 1 bunch of radishes, trimmed and halved
- 1 tablespoon of butter
- 1/2 teaspoon of sea salt

INSTRUCTIONS

1. Preheat the air fryer to 400°F (200°C).
2. In a mixing bowl, toss the halved radishes with melted butter or vegan butter substitute and sea salt.
3. Place the radishes in the air fryer basket and cook for 8-10 minutes, shaking the basket halfway through, until the radishes are tender and slightly charred.
4. Serve hot as a side dish.

Nutrition Information (per serving): Calories 54; Fat 5g; Carbohydrates 2g; Fiber 1g; Protein 1g

Roasted Beets with Orange and Thyme

★ ★ ★ ☆ ☆

COOK TIME: 30 MINUTES

PREP TIME: 10 MINUTES

SERVINGS: 4

INGREDIENTS

- 4 medium beets, peeled and diced
- 2 tablespoons olive oil
- Salt and pepper to taste
- 1 teaspoon fresh thyme leaves
- 1 orange, zested and juiced

INSTRUCTIONS

1. Preheat the air fryer to 375°F (190°C).
2. In a mixing bowl, toss the diced beets with olive oil, salt, pepper, and fresh thyme leaves until well coated.
3. Transfer the coated beets to the air fryer basket and cook for 25-30 minutes or until tender, tossing them halfway through the cooking process.
4. Once the beets are done, transfer them to a mixing bowl and drizzle them with orange juice and zest. Toss to combine.
5. Serve warm or at room temperature.

Nutrition Information (per serving): Calories: 110; Fat: 7g; Carbohydrates: 11g; Fiber: 3g; Protein: 2g

Chapter 5
Desserts

Apple Chips with Cinnamon and Sugar

★★☆☆☆

COOK TIME:
15 MINUTES

PREP TIME:
10 MINUTES

SERVINGS:
4

INGREDIENTS

- 4 medium apples, thinly sliced
- 1 tsp ground cinnamon
- 1 tsp granulated sugar

INSTRUCTIONS

1. Preheat the air fryer to 375°F (190°C).
2. In a small bowl, mix together the cinnamon and sugar.
3. Arrange the sliced apples in a single layer in the air fryer basket.
4. Sprinkle the cinnamon sugar mixture over the apple slices.
5. Air fry for 10 minutes, then flip the apple slices and air fry for an additional 5 minutes, or until crispy and golden brown.
6. Serve immediately.

Nutrition Information (per serving): Calories: 68, Fat: 0.3g, Carbohydrates: 18.1g, Protein: 0.4g, Fiber: 3.2g

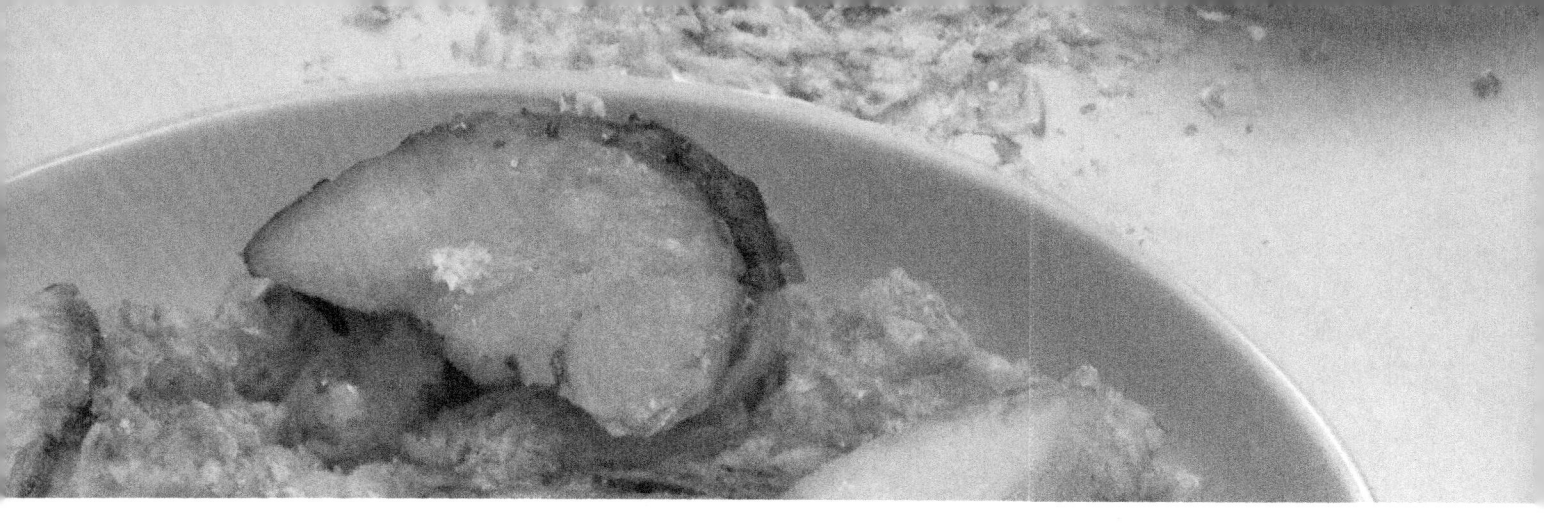

Peach Crisp with Oats and Brown Sugar

★ ★ ★ ☆ ☆

COOK TIME: 20 MINUTES

PREP TIME: 15 MINUTES

SERVINGS: 4

INGREDIENTS

- 4 ripe peaches, sliced
- 1/2 cup rolled oats
- 1/2 cup all-purpose flour
- 1/2 cup brown sugar
- 1/2 tsp cinnamon
- 1/4 tsp salt
- 1/4 cup vegan butter, melted

INSTRUCTIONS

1. Preheat the air fryer to 375°F (190°C).
2. In a mixing bowl, combine the rolled oats, all-purpose flour, brown sugar, cinnamon, salt, and melted vegan butter. Mix until crumbly.
3. Arrange the sliced peaches in a baking dish or air fryer basket.
4. Sprinkle the oat mixture over the peaches, covering them completely.
5. Place the baking dish or air fryer basket into the air fryer and cook for 20 minutes or until the topping is golden brown and the peaches are tender.
6. Serve warm.

Nutrition Information (per serving): Calories: 261, Fat: 8g, Carbohydrates: 47g, Protein: 3g, Fiber: 3g

Baked Banana Bread with Walnuts and Cinnamon

★ ★ ★ ☆ ☆

COOK TIME: 30 MINUTES

PREP TIME: 15 MINUTES

SERVINGS: 4

INGREDIENTS

- 3 ripe bananas, mashed
- 1/4 cup vegetable oil
- 1/4 cup almond milk
- 1/2 cup granulated sugar
- 1 teaspoon vanilla extract
- 1 1/2 cups all-purpose flour
- 1 teaspoon baking soda
- 1/2 teaspoon salt
- 1/2 teaspoon ground cinnamon
- 1/2 cup chopped walnuts

INSTRUCTIONS

1. Preheat the air fryer to 320°F.
2. Grease a small loaf pan that fits inside the air fryer basket.
3. In a large mixing bowl, combine the mashed bananas, vegetable oil, almond milk, sugar, and vanilla extract.
4. In a separate mixing bowl, whisk together the flour, baking soda, salt, and ground cinnamon.
5. Add the dry ingredients to the banana mixture and stir until just combined.
6. Fold in the chopped walnuts.
7. Pour the batter into the prepared loaf pan.
8. Place the loaf pan into the air fryer basket.
9. Air fry for 30 minutes or until a toothpick inserted into the center comes out clean.
10. Let the banana bread cool for 10 minutes before slicing and serving.

Nutrition Information (per serving): Calories 347, Fat 13g, Carbohydrates 54g, Protein 5g, Fiber 3g

Grilled Pineapple with Coconut Sugar and Lime Juice

★ ☆ ☆ ☆ ☆

COOK TIME: 8 MINUTES

PREP TIME: 10 MINUTES

SERVINGS: 4

INGREDIENTS

- 1 pineapple, peeled and cored, cut into rings
- 2 tbsp coconut sugar
- 1 tbsp lime juice
- 1/4 tsp salt

INSTRUCTIONS

1. Preheat the air fryer to 400°F.
2. In a small bowl, mix together the coconut sugar, lime juice, and salt until well combined.
3. Brush both sides of each pineapple ring with the coconut sugar mixture.
4. Place the pineapple rings in the air fryer basket in a single layer.
5. Air fry for 8 minutes, flipping the pineapple rings halfway through the cooking time.
6. Serve hot.

Nutrition Information (per serving): Calories 101, Fat 0.6g, Carbohydrates 26g, Protein 1g, Fiber 2.8g

Cinnamon Sugar Donut Holes with Powdered Sugar

★★☆☆☆

COOK TIME: 8-10 MINUTES

PREP TIME: 10 MINUTES

SERVINGS: 4

INGREDIENTS

- 1 cup all-purpose flour
- 1/4 cup granulated sugar
- 1 teaspoon baking powder
- 1/2 teaspoon ground cinnamon
- 1/4 teaspoon salt
- 1/2 cup unsweetened almond milk
- 1/4 cup unsweetened applesauce
- 1 teaspoon vanilla extract
- 2 tablespoons vegan butter, melted
- 1/2 cup granulated sugar
- 1 teaspoon ground cinnamon
- 1/4 cup powdered sugar

INSTRUCTIONS

1. Preheat the air fryer to 350°F (180°C).
2. In a medium bowl, whisk together the flour, 1/4 cup granulated sugar, baking powder, cinnamon, and salt.
3. In a separate bowl, whisk together the almond milk, applesauce, vanilla extract, and melted vegan butter.
4. Add the wet ingredients to the dry ingredients and stir until just combined.
5. Using a small cookie scoop or spoon, form the dough into 1-inch balls and place them in the air fryer basket.
6. Air fry the dough balls for 8-10 minutes, shaking the basket every 2-3 minutes, until they are golden brown and cooked through.
7. In a small bowl, mix together 1/2 cup granulated sugar and 1 teaspoon ground cinnamon.
8. While the donut holes are still warm, roll them in the cinnamon sugar mixture to coat.
9. Sift powdered sugar over the top of the donut holes before serving.

Nutrition Information (per serving): Calories 266kcal, Fat 5.9g, Carbohydrates 51.8g, Protein 2.9g, Fiber 1.2g

Baked Blueberry Muffins with Almond Flour and Maple Syrup

★★☆☆☆

COOK TIME: 15 MINUTES

PREP TIME: 10 MINUTES

SERVINGS: 6 MUFFINS

INGREDIENTS

- 1 cup almond flour
- 1/2 teaspoon baking soda
- 1/4 teaspoon salt
- 2 tablespoons coconut oil, melted
- 2 tablespoons maple syrup
- 2 flax eggs (2 tablespoons flaxseed meal + 6 tablespoons water)
- 1 teaspoon vanilla extract
- 1/2 cup blueberries

INSTRUCTIONS

1. Preheat the air fryer to 325°F (160°C).
2. In a mixing bowl, whisk together the almond flour, baking soda, and salt.
3. In a separate mixing bowl, whisk together the melted coconut oil, maple syrup, flax eggs, and vanilla extract.
4. Pour the wet ingredients into the dry ingredients and stir until well combined.
5. Gently fold in the blueberries.
6. Scoop the batter into muffin cups, filling each cup about 3/4 full.
7. Place the muffin cups in the air fryer basket and bake for 15 minutes, or until a toothpick inserted into the center of a muffin comes out clean.
8. Let the muffins cool for a few minutes before removing them from the muffin cups..

Nutrition Information (per serving): Calories: 192 kcal; Fat: 16g; Carbohydrates: 10g; Fiber: 3g; Protein: 4g

Sweet Potato Pie with Coconut Oil and Maple Syrup

★ ★ ★ ★ ☆

COOK TIME: 45 MINUTES

PREP TIME: 20 MINUTES

SERVINGS: 8

INGREDIENTS

- 1 unbaked 9-inch pie crust
- 3 cups mashed sweet potatoes
- 3/4 cup maple syrup
- 1/2 cup full-fat coconut milk
- 1/4 cup melted coconut oil
- 2 tablespoons cornstarch
- 1 tablespoon ground cinnamon
- 1/2 teaspoon ground nutmeg
- 1/4 teaspoon ground ginger
- 1/4 teaspoon salt

INSTRUCTIONS

1. Preheat the air fryer to 350°F.
2. In a large mixing bowl, whisk together the mashed sweet potatoes, maple syrup, coconut milk, coconut oil, cornstarch, cinnamon, nutmeg, ginger, and salt until smooth.
3. Pour the filling into the pie crust.
4. Place the pie in the air fryer basket and cook for 45 minutes or until the pie is set and the crust is golden brown.
5. Let the pie cool before serving.

Nutrition Information (per serving): Calories 342, Fat 19g, Carbohydrates 40g, Protein 3g, Fiber 3g

Grilled Peaches with Vanilla Ice Cream and Caramel Sauce

★★☆☆☆

COOK TIME: 10 MINUTES

PREP TIME: 5 MINUTES

SERVINGS: 2

INGREDIENTS

- 2 peaches, halved and pitted
- 1 tbsp brown sugar
- 1/2 tsp ground cinnamon
- 1 tbsp coconut oil, melted
- Vanilla ice cream
- Caramel sauce

INSTRUCTIONS

1. Preheat the air fryer to 375°F (190°C).
2. In a small bowl, mix together the brown sugar and ground cinnamon.
3. Brush the cut side of each peach half with melted coconut oil, then sprinkle the cinnamon sugar mixture over them.
4. Place the peaches in the air fryer basket cut side up and air fry for 8-10 minutes, or until the peaches are softened and slightly caramelized.
5. Serve the grilled peaches with a scoop of vanilla ice cream and a drizzle of caramel sauce.
6. Enjoy!

Nutrition Information (per serving): Calories 87, Fat 4g, Carbohydrates 15g, Protein 1g, Fiber 2g

Cinnamon sugar donuts

★★☆☆☆

COOK TIME: 8 MINUTES

PREP TIME: 15 MINUTES

SERVINGS: 6 DONUTS

INGREDIENTS

- 1 cup flour
- 1/3 cup sugar
- 1 tsp baking powder
- 1/4 tsp baking soda
- 1/4 tsp salt
- 1/2 tsp cinnamon
- 1/3 cup milk
- 1 egg
- 2 tbsp unsalted butter, melted
- 1 tsp vanilla extract
- 1/4 cup sugar
- 1 tsp cinnamon
- 1 tbsp unsalted butter, melted

INSTRUCTIONS

1. In a large bowl, whisk together the flour, sugar, baking powder, baking soda, salt, and cinnamon.
2. In a separate bowl, whisk together the milk, egg, melted butter, and vanilla extract until well combined.
3. Pour the wet ingredients into the dry ingredients and stir until just combined.
4. Spray the air fryer basket with cooking spray and spoon the batter into a piping bag or a large Ziploc bag with the corner cut off.
5. Pipe the batter into the air fryer basket to make 6 donuts.
6. Air fry at 350°F for 8 minutes or until the donuts are golden brown and cooked through.
7. While the donuts are cooking, mix together the sugar and cinnamon for the topping in a shallow bowl.
8. Once the donuts are done, brush them with melted butter and immediately dip them in the cinnamon sugar mixture to coat.

Nutrition Information (per serving): Calories 213, Fat 7g, Carbohydrates 34g, Protein 3g, Fiber 1g

Strawberry Rhubarb Crumble with Almond Flour and Coconut Sugar

★★☆☆☆

COOK TIME:
25-30 MINUTES

PREP TIME:
15 MINUTES

SERVINGS:
4

INGREDIENTS

- 2 cups diced rhubarb
- 2 cups diced strawberries
- 1/2 cup almond flour
- 1/2 cup coconut sugar
- 1/2 cup rolled oats
- 1/4 cup coconut oil
- 1 tsp vanilla extract
- 1/2 tsp cinnamon
- Pinch of salt

INSTRUCTIONS

1. Preheat the air fryer to 350°F (175°C).
2. In a mixing bowl, combine the diced rhubarb and strawberries.
3. In a separate bowl, mix the almond flour, coconut sugar, oats, coconut oil, vanilla extract, cinnamon, and salt until crumbly.
4. Spread the fruit mixture in the bottom of a baking dish that fits in the air fryer.
5. Top the fruit mixture with the crumbly mixture, spreading it evenly.
6. Place the baking dish in the air fryer and cook for 25-30 minutes or until the crumble is golden brown and the fruit is soft and bubbly.
7. Serve warm with vegan ice cream, if desired.

Nutrition Information (per serving): Calories 312, Fat 17g, Carbohydrates 38g, Protein 3g, Fiber 5g

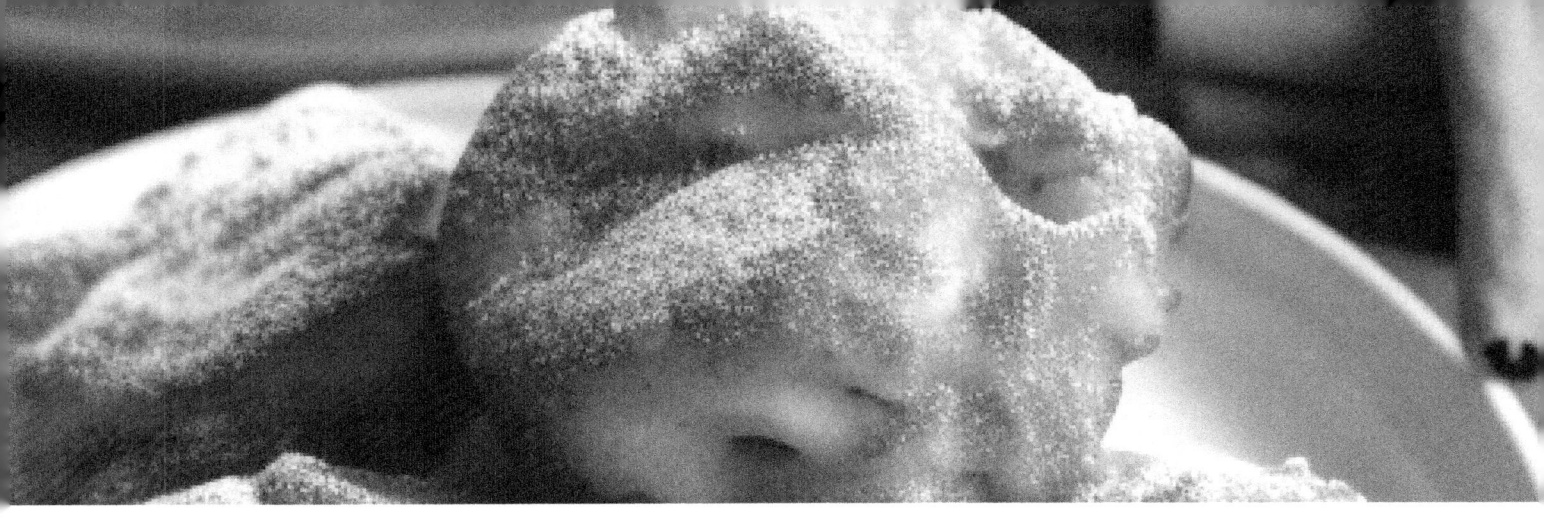

Baked Apple Fritters with Cinnamon and Sugar

★ ★ ☆ ☆ ☆

COOK TIME:
8-10 MINUTES

PREP TIME:
15 MINUTES

SERVINGS:
8 FRITTERS

INGREDIENTS

- 1 cup all-purpose flour
- 1/4 cup granulated sugar
- 1 tsp baking powder
- 1/2 tsp ground cinnamon
- 1/4 tsp salt
- 1/4 cup unsweetened applesauce
- 1/4 cup almond milk
- 1/4 cup vegan butter, melted
- 1 apple, peeled and chopped
- 1/4 cup powdered sugar
- 1/4 tsp ground cinnamon

INSTRUCTIONS

1. Preheat the air fryer to 350°F (175°C).
2. In a large mixing bowl, whisk together the flour, granulated sugar, baking powder, cinnamon, and salt.
3. Add in the applesauce, almond milk, melted vegan butter, and chopped apple. Stir until well combined.
4. Using a cookie scoop, scoop the dough onto a lined air fryer basket.
5. Air fry the fritters for 8-10 minutes or until golden brown.
6. In a small mixing bowl, whisk together the powdered sugar and cinnamon.
7. Remove the fritters from the air fryer and sprinkle the cinnamon sugar mixture over the top of each fritter.

Nutrition Information (per serving): Calories 147, Fat 5g, Carbohydrates 24g, Protein 2g, Fiber 1g

Cinnamon Sugar Churros with Chocolate Sauce

★★★★☆

COOK TIME: 10 MINUTES

PREP TIME: 20 MINUTES

SERVINGS: 4

INGREDIENTS

- 1 cup water
- 1/4 cup vegetable oil
- 1/2 teaspoon salt
- 1 cup all-purpose flour
- 1 tablespoon ground cinnamon
- 1/4 cup granulated sugar
- 1/2 cup vegan chocolate chips
- 1/4 cup non-dairy milk

INSTRUCTIONS

1. Preheat your air fryer to 375°F (190°C).
2. In a saucepan, bring water, vegetable oil, and salt to a boil over medium-high heat.
3. Remove from heat and add flour, stirring until mixture forms a ball.
4. In a separate small bowl, combine cinnamon and sugar.
5. Fill a piping bag fitted with a star tip with the dough.
6. Pipe the dough into 4-inch strips onto a piece of parchment paper, then cut each strip into 2-3 pieces.
7. Place the churros into the air fryer basket in a single layer and air fry for 8-10 minutes, until golden brown and crispy.
8. Toss the churros in the cinnamon sugar mixture.
9. In a small microwave-safe bowl, combine the vegan chocolate chips and non-dairy milk.
10. Microwave on high for 30 seconds, stir until the chocolate has melted and the sauce is smooth.
11. Serve hot with the chocolate sauce for dipping.

Nutrition Information (per serving): Calories 313, Fat 18g, Carbohydrates 34g, Protein 3g, Fiber 3g

CHAPTER 5. DESSERTS

Grilled Nectarines with Ice Cream and Berry Sauce

★★☆☆☆

COOK TIME: 10 MINUTES

PREP TIME: 10 MINUTES

SERVINGS: 4

INGREDIENTS

- 2 ripe nectarines, halved and pitted
- 1 tablespoon coconut oil, melted
- 1 tablespoon honey (or maple syrup for vegan option)
- 1/2 teaspoon cinnamon
- Pinch of sea salt
- 2 scoops vegan vanilla ice cream (or regular vanilla ice cream)
- Fresh berries for garnish

For the Berry Sauce:
- 1/2 cup mixed berries (strawberries, blueberries, raspberries)
- 1 tablespoon honey (or maple syrup for vegan option)
- 1 tablespoon water

INSTRUCTIONS

1. Preheat the air fryer to 350°F.
2. In a small bowl, mix together the melted coconut oil, honey, cinnamon, and salt.
3. Brush the mixture onto the cut side of each nectarine half.
4. Place the nectarines, cut side down, in the air fryer basket.
5. Air fry for 5-6 minutes or until the nectarines are slightly softened and caramelized.
6. Meanwhile, make the berry sauce by blending the berries, honey, and water in a blender until smooth.
7. Serve the grilled nectarines with a scoop of ice cream, drizzle of berry sauce, and fresh berries on top.

Nutrition Information (per serving): Calories 241, Fat 11g, Carbohydrates 36g, Protein 2g, Fiber 3g

Baked Peach Cobbler with Oats and Coconut Sugar

★★✰✰✰

COOK TIME: 20 MINUTES

PREP TIME: 15 MINUTES

SERVINGS: 4

INGREDIENTS

- 4 medium peaches, peeled and sliced
- 1/2 cup rolled oats
- 1/2 cup almond flour
- 1/4 cup coconut sugar
- 1/4 cup vegan butter, melted
- 1 teaspoon ground cinnamon
- 1/4 teaspoon salt

INSTRUCTIONS

1. Preheat the air fryer to 375°F (190°C).
2. In a mixing bowl, combine the sliced peaches with 1 tablespoon of coconut sugar and mix well.
3. In a separate bowl, combine the rolled oats, almond flour, remaining coconut sugar, cinnamon, and salt. Mix well.
4. Add the melted vegan butter to the oat mixture and mix until crumbly.
5. Add the peaches to the air fryer basket and top with the oat mixture.
6. Air fry for 15-20 minutes, or until the topping is golden brown and the peaches are tender.
7. Serve warm, topped with vegan whipped cream or ice cream if desired.

Nutrition Information (per serving): Calories 232, Fat 12g, Carbohydrates 29g, Protein 4g, Fiber 4g

Grilled Plums with Ice Cream and Balsamic Glaze

★ ★ ☆ ☆ ☆

COOK TIME: 10 MINUTES

PREP TIME: 10 MINUTES

SERVINGS: 4

INGREDIENTS

- 2 ripe plums, sliced in half and pitted
- 1 tbsp olive oil
- 1 tbsp balsamic glaze
- 2 scoops vanilla ice cream
- Fresh mint leaves (optional)

INSTRUCTIONS

1. Preheat the air fryer to 380°F (193°C).
2. Brush the plum halves with olive oil on all sides.
3. Place the plum halves in the air fryer basket, cut side down.
4. Air fry for 4-6 minutes, until plums are softened and slightly caramelized.
5. Place the grilled plums on a plate, top with a scoop of vanilla ice cream, and drizzle with balsamic glaze.
6. Garnish with fresh mint leaves if desired.

Nutrition Information (per serving): Calories 192, Fat 10g, Carbohydrates 24g, Protein 3g, Fiber 2g

Cinnamon Sugar Apple Rings with Caramel Dip

★ ☆ ☆ ☆ ☆

COOK TIME: 10 MINUTES

PREP TIME: 10 MINUTES

SERVINGS: 4

INGREDIENTS

- 2 large apples, cored and sliced into rings
- 1/4 cup all-purpose flour
- 1/2 teaspoon ground cinnamon
- 1/4 teaspoon salt
- 1/4 cup unsweetened almond milk
- 1/2 cup breadcrumbs
- 1/4 cup coconut sugar
- Cooking spray
- 1/2 cup vegan caramel sauce

INSTRUCTIONS

1. Preheat air fryer to 370°F (188°C).
2. In a shallow dish, mix together the flour, cinnamon, and salt. Pour the almond milk into another shallow dish.
3. In a third shallow dish, mix together the breadcrumbs and coconut sugar.
4. Dip each apple ring into the flour mixture, shaking off any excess. Next, dip each ring into the almond milk, and finally coat in the breadcrumb mixture.
5. Place the coated apple rings in a single layer in the air fryer basket, lightly spray with cooking spray.
6. Cook for 8-10 minutes or until golden brown, flipping halfway through cooking.
7. Serve hot with vegan caramel sauce for dipping.

Nutrition Information (per serving): Calories 222, Fat 4g, Carbohydrates 47g, Protein 2g, Fiber 4g.

Baked Banana Bread with Chocolate Chips and Walnuts

★★☆☆☆

COOK TIME: 35 MINUTES

PREP TIME: 15 MINUTES

SERVINGS: 8

INGREDIENTS

- 3 ripe bananas, mashed
- 1/3 cup coconut oil, melted
- 1/2 cup coconut sugar
- 1 flax egg (1 tablespoon ground flaxseed mixed with 3 tablespoons water)
- 1 teaspoon vanilla extract
- 1 1/2 cups almond flour
- 1 teaspoon baking soda
- 1/4 teaspoon salt
- 1/2 cup vegan chocolate chips
- 1/2 cup chopped walnuts

INSTRUCTIONS

1. Preheat your air fryer to 320°F (160°C).
2. Grease a 6-inch cake pan that fits inside the air fryer basket.
3. In a mixing bowl, combine the mashed bananas, melted coconut oil, coconut sugar, flax egg, and vanilla extract.
4. Add the almond flour, baking soda, and salt to the bowl and mix until combined.
5. Fold in the chocolate chips and chopped walnuts.
6. Pour the batter into the greased cake pan and smooth out the top.
7. Place the cake pan into the air fryer basket and air fry for 35 minutes or until a toothpick inserted into the center comes out clean.
8. Remove the cake pan from the air fryer and let the banana bread cool for a few minutes before slicing and serving.

Nutrition Information (per serving): Calories 310, Fat 22g, Carbohydrates 26g, Protein 5g, Fiber 4g

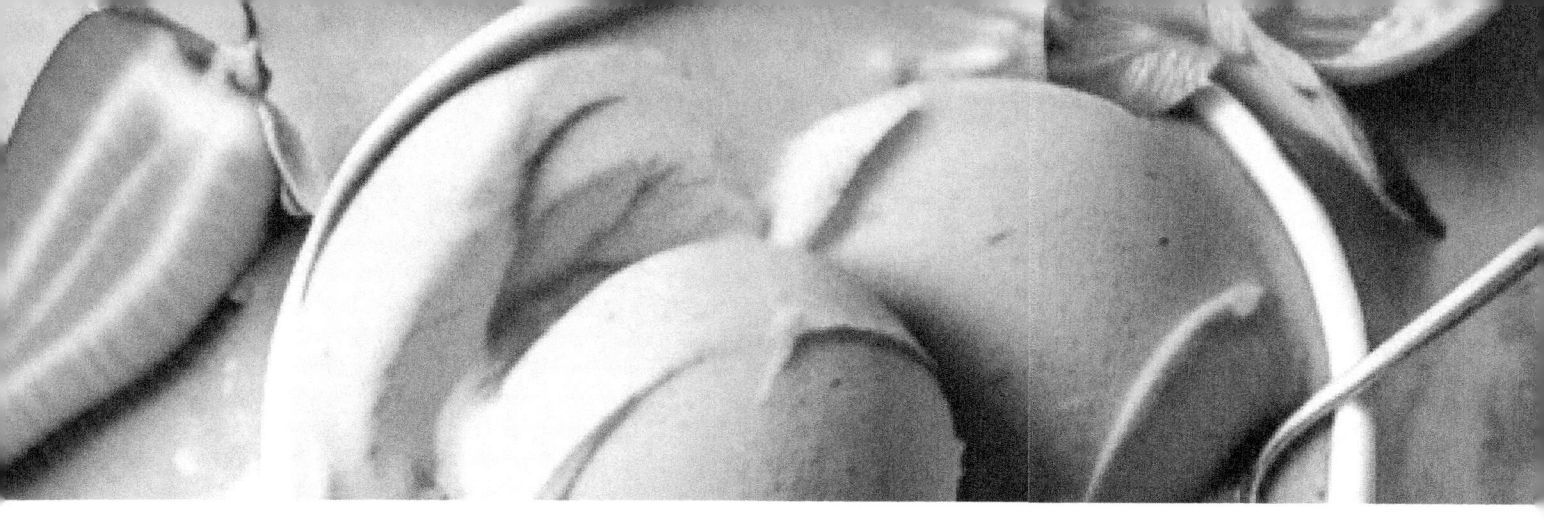

Strawberry Sorbet with Coconut Milk and Sugar

★ ★ ★ ☆ ☆

COOK TIME:
10-15 MINUTES

PREP TIME:
10 MINUTES

SERVINGS:
4

INGREDIENTS

- 1 pound frozen strawberries
- 1/2 cup coconut milk
- 1/4 cup granulated sugar
- 1 tablespoon lemon juice

INSTRUCTIONS

1. Preheat your air fryer to 350°F (175°C).
2. In a blender or food processor, blend the frozen strawberries, coconut milk, sugar, and lemon juice until smooth.
3. Pour the mixture into a freezer-safe container and freeze for about 4-6 hours or until firm.
4. Once the sorbet is frozen, remove it from the freezer and let it sit at room temperature for 10-15 minutes before scooping and serving.

Nutrition Information (per serving): Calories 160, Fat 4g, Carbohydrates 34g, Protein 2g, Fiber 3g

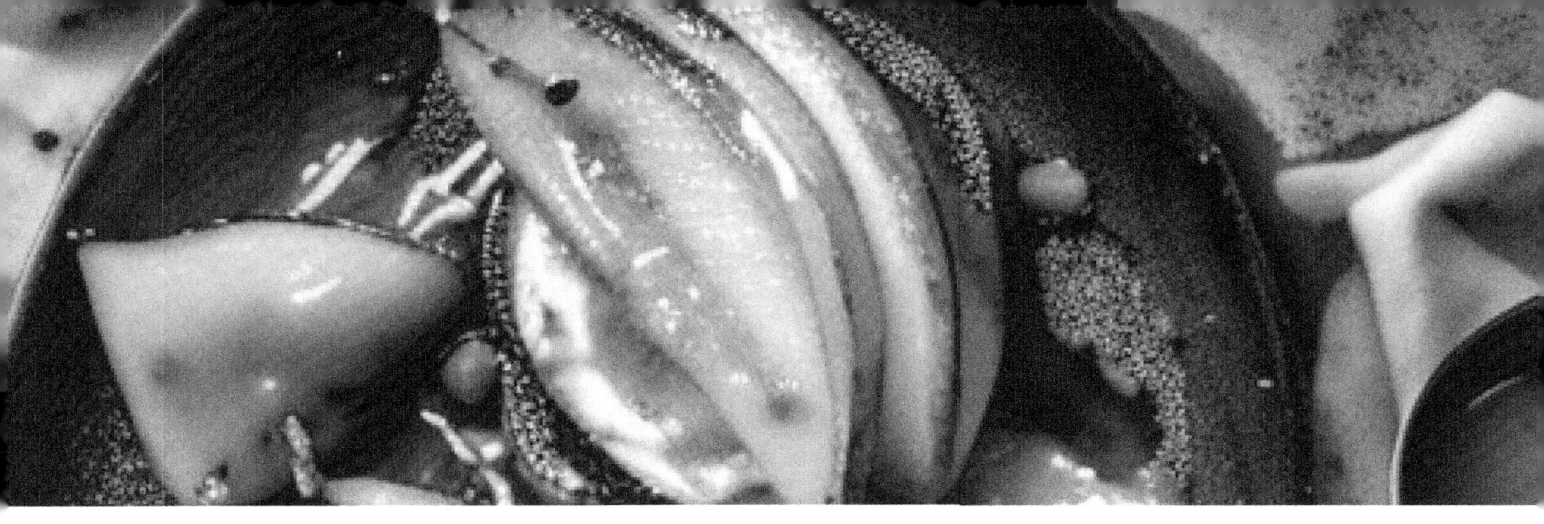

Grilled Pears with Vanilla Ice Cream and Honey

★★✩✩✩

COOK TIME:
8 MINUTES

PREP TIME:
10 MINUTES

SERVINGS:
4

INGREDIENTS

- 2 pears, sliced
- 2 tablespoons honey (or maple syrup for a vegan version)
- 1 teaspoon cinnamon
- 1 teaspoon vanilla extract
- Vanilla ice cream
- Chopped nuts (optional)

INSTRUCTIONS

1. Preheat the air fryer to 375°F (190°C).
2. In a bowl, mix together the honey (or maple syrup), cinnamon, and vanilla extract.
3. Add the sliced pears to the bowl and toss until they are evenly coated in the honey mixture.
4. Place the pears in the air fryer basket and cook for 8 minutes, flipping halfway through.
5. Once done, remove the pears from the air fryer and let them cool for a few minutes.
6. Serve the grilled pears with a scoop of vanilla ice cream (or vegan vanilla ice cream) and sprinkle with chopped nuts (optional).

Nutrition Information (per serving): Calories 167, Fat 2g, Carbohydrates 38g, Protein 1g, Fiber 5g

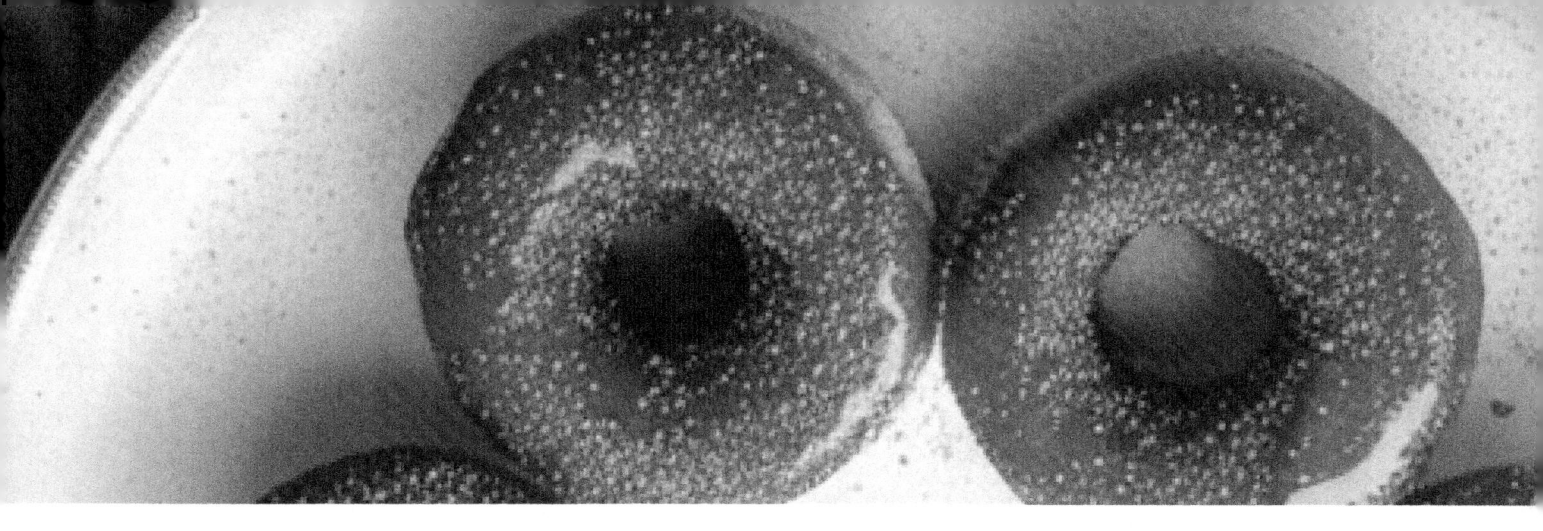

Baked Cinnamon Sugar Donuts with Chocolate Glaze

★★☆☆☆

COOK TIME: 6-8 MINUTES

PREP TIME: 10 MINUTES

SERVINGS: 6 DONUTS

INGREDIENTS

- 1 cup all-purpose flour
- 1/3 cup granulated sugar
- 1 tsp baking powder
- 1/2 tsp baking soda
- 1/2 tsp ground cinnamon
- 1/4 tsp salt
- 1/2 cup unsweetened almond milk
- 1 tsp apple cider vinegar
- 2 tbsp melted coconut oil
- 1 tsp vanilla extract
- 1/4 cup vegan chocolate chips

For the cinnamon sugar coating:
- 1/4 cup granulated sugar
- 1 tsp ground cinnamon

INSTRUCTIONS

1. In a large mixing bowl, whisk together the flour, sugar, baking powder, baking soda, cinnamon, and salt.
2. In a separate bowl, combine the almond milk and apple cider vinegar. Let sit for a few minutes until the mixture curdles.
3. Add the melted coconut oil and vanilla extract to the almond milk mixture and whisk to combine.
4. Pour the wet ingredients into the dry ingredients and stir until just combined.
5. Preheat the air fryer to 350°F.
6. Lightly grease the air fryer basket with cooking spray.
7. Use a piping bag or spoon to fill the donut molds with the batter.
8. Air fry for 6-8 minutes or until the donuts are golden brown and a toothpick comes out clean.
9. While the donuts are still warm, mix together the granulated sugar and ground cinnamon for the coating.
10. Dip each donut into the cinnamon sugar mixture to coat.
11. Melt the chocolate chips in the microwave or on a stovetop double boiler.
12. Drizzle the melted chocolate over the donuts.

Nutrition Information (per serving): Calories 243kcal, Fat 9g, Carbohydrates 38g, Protein 3g, Fiber 1g

Grilled Mangoes with Ice Cream and Coconut Milk

★★☆☆☆

COOK TIME: 10 MINUTES

PREP TIME: 10 MINUTES

SERVINGS: 2

INGREDIENTS

- 1 ripe mango, sliced
- 1 tbsp coconut oil, melted
- 1 tbsp brown sugar
- 1/2 tsp ground cinnamon
- 1/4 cup coconut milk
- 2 scoops of vegan vanilla ice cream

INSTRUCTIONS

1. Preheat the air fryer to 375°F (190°C).
2. In a small bowl, mix together the melted coconut oil, brown sugar, and ground cinnamon.
3. Brush the mixture onto the mango slices.
4. Place the mango slices into the air fryer basket and cook for 8-10 minutes, flipping once halfway through.
5. Serve the grilled mango slices with a scoop of vegan vanilla ice cream and a drizzle of coconut milk.

Nutrition Information (per serving): Calories 208, Fat 12g, Carbohydrates 26g, Protein 2g, Fiber 2g.

100 Daily Meal Plan

	BREAKFAST	LUNCH	DINNER
1	Avocado Toast with Vegan Feta Cheese	Vegan Grilled Cheese Sandwich	Teriyaki Tofu and Vegetables with Rice
2	Bake with Tofu and Broccoli	BBQ Tofu and Vegetable Skewers with Barbecue Sauce	Zucchini and Tomato Gratin with Vegan Cheese and Herbs
3	Baked Oatmeal with Nuts and Dried Fruit	Butternut Squash and Sage Lasagna with Vegan Cheese	Vegan Grilled Cheese Sandwich
4	Bowl with Tofu Scramble and Roasted Veggies	Cauliflower Steaks with Romesco Sauce and Almonds	Tofu and Vegetable Stir-Fry with Sesame Oil and Soy Sauce
5	Breakfast Casserole with Tofu and Vegetables	Chickpea and Vegetable Burgers with Buns and Fixings	BBQ Tofu and Vegetable Skewers with Barbecue Sauce
6	Burrito with Tofu Scramble	Chickpea Curry with Coconut Milk and Spices	Sweet Potato and Kale Enchiladas with Red Sauce and Vegan Cheese
7	French Toast Casserole with Cinnamon and Maple Syrup	Lentil and Vegetable Shepherd's Pie with Mashed Potatoes	Sweet Potato and Black Bean Tacos with Avocado Cream Sauce
8	French Toast with Berry Compote	Mushroom and Onion Pizzas with Vegan Cheese and Herbs	Stuffed Portobello Mushrooms with Quinoa, Spinach and Vegan Cheese
9	Frittata with Spinach and Tomatoes	Pad Thai with Rice Noodles and Peanut Sauce	Stuffed Bell Peppers with Quinoa, Black Beans and Vegan Cheese
10	Pancakes with Blueberries	Quinoa and Vegetable Bowl with Lemon and Olive Oil	Seitan and Vegetable Skewers with Lemon and Herbs
11	Potatoes with Rosemary and Garlic	Ratatouille with Tomato Sauce and Herbs	Roasted Vegetable and Rice Casserole with Vegan Cheese
12	Quesadilla with Spinach and Mushroom	Roasted Vegetable and Rice Casserole with Vegan Cheese	Cauliflower Steaks with Romesco Sauce and Almonds
13	Sandwiches with Veggie Bacon	Seitan and Vegetable Skewers with Lemon and Herbs	Quinoa and Vegetable Bowl with Lemon and Olive Oil
14	Sausage Patties	Stuffed Bell Peppers with Quinoa, Black Beans and Vegan Cheese	Pad Thai with Rice Noodles and Peanut Sauce
15	Strata with Grilled Veggies	Stuffed Portobello Mushrooms with Quinoa, Spinach and Vegan Cheese	Mushroom and Onion Pizzas with Vegan Cheese and Herbs

16	Stuffed Peppers with Quinoa and Black Beans	Sweet Potato and Black Bean Tacos with Avocado Cream Sauce	Lentil and Vegetable Shepherd's Pie with Mashed Potatoes
17	Sweet Potato Hash with Kale and Chickpeas	Sweet Potato and Kale Enchiladas with Red Sauce and Vegan Cheese	Chickpea Curry with Coconut Milk and Spices
18	Sweet Potato Waffles with Maple Syrup	Teriyaki Tofu and Vegetables with Rice	Chickpea and Vegetable Burgers with Buns and Fixings
19	Tacos with Tofu Scramble and Salsa	Tofu and Vegetable Stir-Fry with Sesame Oil and Soy Sauce	Cauliflower Steaks with Romesco Sauce and Almonds
20	Waffles with Fresh Fruit	Vegan Grilled Cheese Sandwich	Butternut Squash and Sage Lasagna with Vegan Cheese
21	Avocado Toast with Vegan Feta Cheese	Zucchini and Tomato Gratin with Vegan Cheese and Herbs	BBQ Tofu and Vegetable Skewers with Barbecue Sauce
22	Strata with Grilled Veggies	Chickpea and Vegetable Burgers with Buns and Fixings	Ratatouille with Tomato Sauce and Herbs
23	Sausage Patties	Seitan and Vegetable Skewers with Lemon and Herbs	Chickpea Curry with Coconut Milk and Spices
24	Sandwiches with Veggie Bacon	Roasted Vegetable and Rice Casserole with Vegan Cheese	Tofu and Vegetable Stir-Fry with Sesame Oil and Soy Sauce
25	Quesadilla with Spinach and Mushroom	Ratatouille with Tomato Sauce and Herbs	Teriyaki Tofu and Vegetables with Rice
26	Potatoes with Rosemary and Garlic	Quinoa and Vegetable Bowl with Lemon and Olive Oil	Sweet Potato and Kale Enchiladas with Red Sauce and Vegan Cheese
27	Pancakes with Blueberries	Pad Thai with Rice Noodles and Peanut Sauce	Sweet Potato and Black Bean Tacos with Avocado Cream Sauce
28	Frittata with Spinach and Tomatoes	Mushroom and Onion Pizzas with Vegan Cheese and Herbs	Stuffed Portobello Mushrooms with Quinoa, Spinach and Vegan Cheese
29	French Toast with Berry Compote	Lentil and Vegetable Shepherd's Pie with Mashed Potatoes	Stuffed Bell Peppers with Quinoa, Black Beans and Vegan Cheese
30	Tacos with Tofu Scramble and Salsa	Chickpea Curry with Coconut Milk and Spices	Pad Thai with Rice Noodles and Peanut Sauce

31	Stuffed Peppers with Quinoa and Black Beans	Vegan Grilled Cheese Sandwich	Roasted Vegetable and Rice Casserole with Vegan Cheese
32	Sweet Potato Hash with Kale and Chickpeas	BBQ Tofu and Vegetable Skewers with Barbecue Sauce	Cauliflower Steaks with Romesco Sauce and Almonds
33	Sweet Potato Waffles with Maple Syrup	Butternut Squash and Sage Lasagna with Vegan Cheese	Quinoa and Vegetable Bowl with Lemon and Olive Oil
34	Tacos with Tofu Scramble and Salsa	Cauliflower Steaks with Romesco Sauce and Almonds	Pad Thai with Rice Noodles and Peanut Sauce
35	Waffles with Fresh Fruit	Chickpea and Vegetable Burgers with Buns and Fixings	Mushroom and Onion Pizzas with Vegan Cheese and Herbs
36	Avocado Toast with Vegan Feta Cheese	Chickpea Curry with Coconut Milk and Spices	Lentil and Vegetable Shepherd's Pie with Mashed Potatoes
37	Strata with Grilled Veggies	Lentil and Vegetable Shepherd's Pie with Mashed Potatoes	Chickpea Curry with Coconut Milk and Spices
38	Sausage Patties	Mushroom and Onion Pizzas with Vegan Cheese and Herbs	Chickpea and Vegetable Burgers with Buns and Fixings
39	Sandwiches with Veggie Bacon	Pad Thai with Rice Noodles and Peanut Sauce	Cauliflower Steaks with Romesco Sauce and Almonds
40	Quesadilla with Spinach and Mushroom	Quinoa and Vegetable Bowl with Lemon and Olive Oil	Butternut Squash and Sage Lasagna with Vegan Cheese
41	Potatoes with Rosemary and Garlic	Ratatouille with Tomato Sauce and Herbs	BBQ Tofu and Vegetable Skewers with Barbecue Sauce
42	Pancakes with Blueberries	Roasted Vegetable and Rice Casserole with Vegan Cheese	Ratatouille with Tomato Sauce and Herbs
43	Frittata with Spinach and Tomatoes	Seitan and Vegetable Skewers with Lemon and Herbs	Chickpea Curry with Coconut Milk and Spices
44	French Toast with Berry Compote	Stuffed Bell Peppers with Quinoa, Black Beans and Vegan Cheese	Tofu and Vegetable Stir-Fry with Sesame Oil and Soy Sauce
45	Tacos with Tofu Scramble and Salsa	Stuffed Portobello Mushrooms with Quinoa, Spinach and Vegan Cheese	Teriyaki Tofu and Vegetables with Rice

46	Avocado Toast with Vegan Feta Cheese	Chickpea Curry with Coconut Milk and Spices	Lentil and Vegetable Shepherd's Pie with Mashed Potatoes
47	Strata with Grilled Veggies	Lentil and Vegetable Shepherd's Pie with Mashed Potatoes	Chickpea Curry with Coconut Milk and Spices
48	Sausage Patties	Mushroom and Onion Pizzas with Vegan Cheese and Herbs	Chickpea and Vegetable Burgers with Buns and Fixings
49	Sandwiches with Veggie Bacon	Pad Thai with Rice Noodles and Peanut Sauce	Cauliflower Steaks with Romesco Sauce and Almonds
50	Quesadilla with Spinach and Mushroom	Quinoa and Vegetable Bowl with Lemon and Olive Oil	Butternut Squash and Sage Lasagna with Vegan Cheese
51	Potatoes with Rosemary and Garlic	Ratatouille with Tomato Sauce and Herbs	BBQ Tofu and Vegetable Skewers with Barbecue Sauce
52	Pancakes with Blueberries	Roasted Vegetable and Rice Casserole with Vegan Cheese	Ratatouille with Tomato Sauce and Herbs
53	Frittata with Spinach and Tomatoes	Seitan and Vegetable Skewers with Lemon and Herbs	Chickpea Curry with Coconut Milk and Spices
54	French Toast with Berry Compote	Stuffed Bell Peppers with Quinoa, Black Beans and Vegan Cheese	Tofu and Vegetable Stir-Fry with Sesame Oil and Soy Sauce
55	Tacos with Tofu Scramble and Salsa	Stuffed Portobello Mushrooms with Quinoa, Spinach and Vegan Cheese	Teriyaki Tofu and Vegetables with Rice
56	Stuffed Peppers with Quinoa and Black Beans	Sweet Potato and Black Bean Tacos with Avocado Cream Sauce	Sweet Potato and Kale Enchiladas with Red Sauce and Vegan Cheese
57	Sweet Potato Hash with Kale and Chickpeas	Sweet Potato and Kale Enchiladas with Red Sauce and Vegan Cheese	Sweet Potato and Black Bean Tacos with Avocado Cream Sauce
58	Sweet Potato Waffles with Maple Syrup	Teriyaki Tofu and Vegetables with Rice	Stuffed Portobello Mushrooms with Quinoa, Spinach and Vegan Cheese
59	Tacos with Tofu Scramble and Salsa	Tofu and Vegetable Stir-Fry with Sesame Oil and Soy Sauce	Stuffed Bell Peppers with Quinoa, Black Beans and Vegan Cheese
60	Waffles with Fresh Fruit	Vegan Grilled Cheese Sandwich	Pad Thai with Rice Noodles and Peanut Sauce

61	Avocado Toast with Vegan Feta Cheese	Zucchini and Tomato Gratin with Vegan Cheese and Herbs	Roasted Vegetable and Rice Casserole with Vegan Cheese
62	Strata with Grilled Veggies	Chickpea and Vegetable Burgers with Buns and Fixings	Cauliflower Steaks with Romesco Sauce and Almonds
63	Sausage Patties	Seitan and Vegetable Skewers with Lemon and Herbs	Quinoa and Vegetable Bowl with Lemon and Olive Oil
64	Sandwiches with Veggie Bacon	Roasted Vegetable and Rice Casserole with Vegan Cheese	Pad Thai with Rice Noodles and Peanut Sauce
65	Quesadilla with Spinach and Mushroom	Ratatouille with Tomato Sauce and Herbs	Mushroom and Onion Pizzas with Vegan Cheese and Herbs
66	Stuffed Peppers with Quinoa and Black Beans	Quinoa and Vegetable Bowl with Lemon and Olive Oil	Roasted Vegetable and Rice Casserole with Vegan Cheese
67	Sweet Potato Hash with Kale and Chickpeas	Pad Thai with Rice Noodles and Peanut Sauce	Cauliflower Steaks with Romesco Sauce and Almonds
68	Sweet Potato Waffles with Maple Syrup	Mushroom and Onion Pizzas with Vegan Cheese and Herbs	Quinoa and Vegetable Bowl with Lemon and Olive Oil
69	Tacos with Tofu Scramble and Salsa	Lentil and Vegetable Shepherd's Pie with Mashed Potatoes	Pad Thai with Rice Noodles and Peanut Sauce
70	Waffles with Fresh Fruit	Chickpea Curry with Coconut Milk and Spices	Mushroom and Onion Pizzas with Vegan Cheese and Herbs
71	Avocado Toast with Vegan Feta Cheese	Vegan Grilled Cheese Sandwich	Lentil and Vegetable Shepherd's Pie with Mashed Potatoes
72	Strata with Grilled Veggies	BBQ Tofu and Vegetable Skewers with Barbecue Sauce	Chickpea Curry with Coconut Milk and Spices
73	Sausage Patties	Butternut Squash and Sage Lasagna with Vegan Cheese	Chickpea and Vegetable Burgers with Buns and Fixings
74	Sandwiches with Veggie Bacon	Cauliflower Steaks with Romesco Sauce and Almonds	Cauliflower Steaks with Romesco Sauce and Almonds
75	Quesadilla with Spinach and Mushroom	Chickpea and Vegetable Burgers with Buns and Fixings	Butternut Squash and Sage Lasagna with Vegan Cheese

76	Potatoes with Rosemary and Garlic	Vegan Grilled Cheese Sandwich	BBQ Tofu and Vegetable Skewers with Barbecue Sauce
77	Pancakes with Blueberries	BBQ Tofu and Vegetable Skewers with Barbecue Sauce	Ratatouille with Tomato Sauce and Herbs
78	Frittata with Spinach and Tomatoes	Butternut Squash and Sage Lasagna with Vegan Cheese	Chickpea Curry with Coconut Milk and Spices
79	French Toast with Berry Compote	Cauliflower Steaks with Romesco Sauce and Almonds	Tofu and Vegetable Stir-Fry with Sesame Oil and Soy Sauce
80	Tacos with Tofu Scramble and Salsa	Chickpea and Vegetable Burgers with Buns and Fixings	Teriyaki Tofu and Vegetables with Rice
81	Avocado Toast with Vegan Feta Cheese	Chickpea Curry with Coconut Milk and Spices	Lentil and Vegetable Shepherd's Pie with Mashed Potatoes
82	Bake with Tofu and Broccoli	Lentil and Vegetable Shepherd's Pie with Mashed Potatoes	Chickpea Curry with Coconut Milk and Spices
83	Baked Oatmeal with Nuts and Dried Fruit	Mushroom and Onion Pizzas with Vegan Cheese and Herbs	Chickpea and Vegetable Burgers with Buns and Fixings
84	Bowl with Tofu Scramble and Roasted Veggies	Pad Thai with Rice Noodles and Peanut Sauce	Cauliflower Steaks with Romesco Sauce and Almonds
85	Breakfast Casserole with Tofu and Vegetables	Quinoa and Vegetable Bowl with Lemon and Olive Oil	Butternut Squash and Sage Lasagna with Vegan Cheese
86	Burrito with Tofu Scramble	Ratatouille with Tomato Sauce and Herbs	BBQ Tofu and Vegetable Skewers with Barbecue Sauce
87	French Toast Casserole with Cinnamon and Maple Syrup	Roasted Vegetable and Rice Casserole with Vegan Cheese	Ratatouille with Tomato Sauce and Herbs
88	French Toast with Berry Compote	Seitan and Vegetable Skewers with Lemon and Herbs	Chickpea Curry with Coconut Milk and Spices
89	Frittata with Spinach and Tomatoes	Stuffed Bell Peppers with Quinoa, Black Beans and Vegan Cheese	Tofu and Vegetable Stir-Fry with Sesame Oil and Soy Sauce
90	Pancakes with Blueberries	Stuffed Portobello Mushrooms with Quinoa, Spinach and Vegan Cheese	Teriyaki Tofu and Vegetables with Rice

91	Potatoes with Rosemary and Garlic	Sweet Potato and Black Bean Tacos with Avocado Cream Sauce	Sweet Potato and Kale Enchiladas with Red Sauce and Vegan Cheese
92	Quesadilla with Spinach and Mushroom	Sweet Potato and Kale Enchiladas with Red Sauce and Vegan Cheese	Sweet Potato and Black Bean Tacos with Avocado Cream Sauce
93	Sandwiches with Veggie Bacon	Teriyaki Tofu and Vegetables with Rice	Stuffed Portobello Mushrooms with Quinoa, Spinach and Vegan Cheese
94	Sausage Patties	Tofu and Vegetable Stir-Fry with Sesame Oil and Soy Sauce	Stuffed Bell Peppers with Quinoa, Black Beans and Vegan Cheese
95	Strata with Grilled Veggies	Vegan Grilled Cheese Sandwich	Pad Thai with Rice Noodles and Peanut Sauce
96	Stuffed Peppers with Quinoa and Black Beans	Zucchini and Tomato Gratin with Vegan Cheese and Herbs	Roasted Vegetable and Rice Casserole with Vegan Cheese
97	Sweet Potato Hash with Kale and Chickpeas	Chickpea and Vegetable Burgers with Buns and Fixings	Cauliflower Steaks with Romesco Sauce and Almonds
98	Sweet Potato Waffles with Maple Syrup	Seitan and Vegetable Skewers with Lemon and Herbs	Quinoa and Vegetable Bowl with Lemon and Olive Oil
99	Tacos with Tofu Scramble and Salsa	Roasted Vegetable and Rice Casserole with Vegan Cheese	Pad Thai with Rice Noodles and Peanut Sauce
100	Waffles with Fresh Fruit	Chickpea and Vegetable Burgers with Buns and Fixings	Chickpea Curry with Coconut Milk and Spices

Measurement Conversion

1 cup	16 tablespoons
1 cup	48 teaspoons
1 tablespoon	3 teaspoons
1 fluid ounce	2 tablespoons
1 pint	2 cups
1 quart	2 pints
1 gallon	4 quarts
1 ounce	28.35 grams
1 pound	16 ounces
1 pound	453.59 grams
1 kilogram	2.20462 pounds
100 °C	212 °F
180 °C	356 °F
250 °C	482 °F

Note: To convert Celsius (°C) to Fahrenheit (°F), multiply the temperature in Celsius by 1.8 and then add 32. To convert Fahrenheit to Celsius, subtract 32 from the temperature in Fahrenheit and then divide by 1.8.

Index of Recipes

A

Apple Chips with Cinnamon and Sugar: 105
Artichoke Hearts with Lemon and Garlic: 53
Avocado Toast with Vegan Feta Cheese: 21

B

Baked Apple Fritters with Cinnamon and Sugar: 115
Baked Banana Bread with Chocolate Chips and Walnuts: 121
Baked Banana Bread with Walnuts and Cinnamon: 107
Baked Blueberry Muffins with Almond Flour and Maple Syrup: 110
Baked Cinnamon Sugar Donuts with Chocolate Glaze: 124
Baked Mac and Cheese Bites with Panko Breadcrumbs: 61
Baked Oatmeal with Nuts and Dried Fruit: 31
Baked Peach Cobbler with Oats and Coconut Sugar: 118
Baked Potato Wedges with Rosemary and Sea Salt: 86
Baked Sweet Potato Rounds with Cinnamon and Maple Syrup: 56
Baked Sweet Potato with Cinnamon and Coconut Oil: 92
Bake with Tofu and Broccoli: 37
BBQ Tofu and Vegetable Skewers with Barbecue Sauce: 75
Bowl with Tofu Scramble and Roasted Veggies: 40
Breakfast Casserole with Tofu and Vegetables: 33
Brussels Sprouts with Balsamic Vinegar and Honey: 50
Burrito with Tofu Scramble: 25
Butternut Squash and Sage Lasagna with Vegan Cheese: 80

C

Carrot Fries with Curry Powder and Coconut Oil: 46
Cauliflower Rice with Turmeric and Cumin: 90
Cauliflower Steaks with Romesco Sauce and Almonds: 70
Cauliflower Wings with Barbecue Sauce: 51
Chickpea and Vegetable Burgers with Buns and Fixings: 81
Chickpea Curry with Coconut Milk and Spices: 65
Cinnamon Sugar Apple Rings with Caramel Dip: 120
Cinnamon Sugar Churros with Chocolate Sauce: 116
Cinnamon Sugar Donut Holes with Powdered Sugar: 109
Cinnamon sugar donuts: 113
Coleslaw with Vegan Mayo and Vinegar: 98

E

Eggplant Parmesan Bites with Marinara Sauce and Vegan Cheese: 57

F

Falafel with Tahini Sauce: 45
French Toast Casserole with Cinnamon and Maple Syrup: 39
French Toast with Berry Compote: 24
Fried Rice Balls with Vegetables and Tamari: 59
Fried Rice with Vegetables and Soy Sauce: 94
Frittata with Spinach and Tomatoes: 38

G

Grilled Asparagus with Lemon and Olive Oil: 89
Grilled Cheese Sandwich: 78
Grilled Corn on the Cob with Chili Powder and Lime: 85
Grilled Eggplant with Balsamic Vinegar and Mint: 97
Grilled Mangoes with Ice Cream and Coconut Milk: 125
Grilled Nectarines with Ice Cream and Berry Sauce: 117
Grilled Peaches with Cinnamon and Honey: 100
Grilled Peaches with Vanilla Ice Cream and Caramel Sauce: 112
Grilled Pears with Vanilla Ice Cream and Honey: 123
Grilled Pineapple with Coconut Sugar and Lime Juice: 108
Grilled Plums with Ice Cream and Balsamic Glaze: 119
Grilled Zucchini with Balsamic Vinegar and Basil: 93

L

Lentil and Vegetable Shepherd's Pie with Mashed Potatoes: 77

M

Mushroom and Onion Pizzas with Vegan Cheese and Herbs: 71

O

Onion Rings with Spicy Dipping Sauce: 43

P

Pad Thai with Rice Noodles and Peanut Sauce: 73
Pancakes with Blueberries: 22
Pasta Salad with Vegetables and Vinaigrette: 99
Peach Crisp with Oats and Brown Sugar: 106
Portobello Mushroom Caps with Balsamic Glaze: 48

Potatoes with Rosemary and Garlic: 30
Potato Salad with Vegan Mayo and Herbs: 101

Q

Quesadilla with Spinach and Mushroom: 26
Quinoa and Vegetable Bowl with Lemon and Olive Oil: 66
Quinoa Salad with Avocado, Cilantro, and Lime: 96

R

Ratatouille with Tomato Sauce and Herbs: 67
Roasted Beets with Orange and Thyme: 103
Roasted Bell Peppers with Oregano and Garlic : 95
Roasted Brussels Sprouts with Balsamic Vinegar and Maple Syrup: 87
Roasted Butternut Squash with Cinnamon and Maple Syrup: 91
Roasted Carrots with Honey and Thyme: 84
Roasted Garlic with Olive Oil and Sea Salt: 58
Roasted Radishes with Butter and Sea Salt: 102
Roasted Vegetable and Rice Casserole with Vegan Cheese: 68

S

Sandwiches with Veggie Bacon: 28
Sausage Patties: 27
Seitan and Vegetable Skewers with Lemon and Herbs: 79
Spiced Chickpeas with Cumin and Paprika: 54
Spiced Nuts with Cayenne and Maple Syrup: 60
Spring Rolls with Sweet and Sour Sauce: 47
Strata with Grilled Veggies: 35
Strawberry Rhubarb Crumble with Almond Flour and Coconut Sugar: 114
Strawberry Sorbet with Coconut Milk and Sugar: 122
Stuffed Bell Peppers with Quinoa, Black Beans and Cheese: 76
Stuffed Jalapenos with Cream Cheese and Chives: 55
Stuffed Peppers with Quinoa and Black Beans: 32
Stuffed Portobello Mushrooms with Quinoa, Spinach and Vegan Cheese: 82
Sweet and Spicy Peppers with Vinegar and Honey: 52
Sweet Potato and Black Bean Tacos with Avocado Cream Sauce: 64
Sweet Potato and Kale Enchiladas with Red Sauce and Vegan Cheese: 72
Sweet Potato Fries with Garlic Aioli: 88
Sweet Potato Fries with Rosemary and Sea Salt: 42
Sweet Potato Hash with Kale and Chickpeas: 23
Sweet Potato Pie with Coconut Oil and Maple Syrup: 111
Sweet Potato Waffles with Maple Syrup: 36

T

Tacos with Tofu Scramble and Salsa: 34
Teriyaki Tofu and Vegetables with Rice: 69
Tofu and Vegetable Stir-Fry with Sesame Oil and Soy Sauce: 63
Tofu Bites with Buffalo Sauce and Ranch Dipping Sauce: 49

W

Waffles with Fresh Fruit: 29

Z

Zucchini and Tomato Gratin with Cheese and Herbs: 74
Zucchini Chips with Parmesan and Herbs: 44

Conclusion

The Plant-Based Air Fryer Cookbook is a definitive guide for anyone who wants to adopt a healthier, plant-based lifestyle. With easy-to-follow recipes and its comprehensive meal plan, this cookbook gives you all the information you need to make quick, delicious, and healthy meals using your air fryer.

The book is divided into two parts: the first part features over 100 plant-based recipes, easy to make, and perfect for everyday cooking. In this cookbook, you'll find something for everyone from appetizers to main dishes, and even desserts. Each recipe includes a list of ingredients, step-by-step instructions, and nutritional information.

The last part of the book is a 30-day meal plan, taking the guesswork out of meal planning. This plan provides a balanced, plant-based diet that is both tasty and nutritious. The recipes included in this plan are all designed to be quick and easy to make, perfect for busy weeknights or lazy weekends.

The air fryer is the real star of this cookbook! Air fryers are your healthier alternative to deep frying, and are used for cooking many foods, from crispy vegetables to juicy burgers. The recipes in this cookbook are designed to benefit from the air fryer's unique cooking properties, resulting in delicious, healthy meals cooked to perfection.

Overall, the Plant-Based Air Fryer Cookbook is a must-have for anyone looking to adopt a plant-based lifestyle. With easy-to-follow recipes, an extensive meal plan, and the use of the air fryer, this cookbook gives you everything you need to make quick, delicious, and healthy meals to satisfy even the most demanding taste buds.

Tips for Successful Plant-Based Air Fryer Cooking

Air fryers have revolutionized the way we cook, especially for those following a plant-based diet. With these appliances, we can cook our favorite dishes using less oil, faster than traditional cooking methods. If you're new to air frying, we'll repeat the vital tips for successful plant-based air fryer cooking.

Remember to preheat your air fryer. This crucial first step ensures the air fryer is at the correct cooking temperature and stops food from sticking to the basket. This is vital when making recipes where the crispy texture is essential, like French fries or onion rings.

Use cooking spray or an oil sprayer to coat your food lightly before air frying. This is the secret to getting a crisp texture and reducing the quantity of oil needed for cooking. And, when choosing an oil, opt for a healthier plant-based variety, like olive or avocado oil.

Finally, experiment! Don't be afraid to try different flavors and spices in your air fryer dishes. You can create a variety of delicious plant-based meals using the air fryer, from veggie burgers to crunchy tofu. Add your favorite spices or seasonings to your dishes and see how this enhances the flavor.

Ultimately, the plant-based air fryer cookbook is a wonderful resource for those of us trying to include healthier cooking methods in our diet. With its bonus 365-day meal plan, it offers plenty of plant-based recipes that are both delicious and easy to make. By following these guidelines for successful plant-based air fryer cooking, you can create endless healthy, flavorful dishes with your air fryer.

Final Thoughts

We believe the Plant-Based Air Fryer Cookbook is a valuable resource for anyone wanting to explore the world of plant-based cooking. The recipes are quick, healthy, and delicious, making it easy to maintain a balanced, nutrient-rich diet. Who doesn't enjoy the taste and texture of fried foods? Using an air fryer, you can have the same taste sensation without all the unhealthy oils and fats.

This cookbook has a wealth of knowledge and inspiration for plant-based meals, both satisfying and nutritious. With a bonus 365-day meal plan, you can easily work these recipes into your daily routine and know you're getting a balanced diet.

Overall, the Plant-Based Air Fryer Cookbook is a must-have for anyone wanting to eat healthier and live more sustainably, while enjoying delicious, plant-based meals. If you're a vegan veteran or just beginning your plant-based journey, this cookbook offers inspiration and delight along the way.

Printed in Great Britain
by Amazon